best new poets

2008

MARK STRAND, EDITOR

Jeb Livingood, Series Editor

This book was published by Samovar Press, LLC, Charlottesville, Virginia,
in cooperation with *Meridian,* www.readmeridian.org. For additional information
on *Best New Poets,* see our Web site at www.bestnewpoets.org.

Cover photograph from Crestock.com

Text set in Adobe Garamond Pro

Printed by Thomson-Shore, Dexter, Michigan

ISBN 13: 978-0-9766296-3-4
ISBN 10: 0-9766296-3-1
ISSN 1554-7019

In memory of George Garrett

Contents

Introduction

Welcome to *Best New Poets 2008,* our fourth installment of fifty poems from emerging writers. In these pages, the term "emerging writer" has a narrow definition: here, it means someone who has yet to publish a book-length collection of poetry. Like the rules for many anthologies, that one is, perhaps, arbitrary. But the main goal of *Best New Poets* is to provide special encouragement and recognition to new poets, the many writing programs they attend, and the magazines that publish their work. And, of course, to deliver an accessible, eclectic sampling of emerging poets to you, the reader.

From April to June of 2008, *Best New Poets* accepted nominations from each of the above sources. For a small reading fee, writers could upload two poems to a Web site, www.bestnewpoets.org, as part of our Open Competition. A month earlier, writing programs from around the United States and Canada had sent nominations of up to two writers, whom *Best New Poets* later solicited for work. And the anthology also asked literary magazines across North America to send two of their best recent poems by writers who met our definition of "emerging." We asked that the poems submitted either be unpublished or published after April 15, 2007. So, not only do new writers appear in this anthology, you're also seeing some of their latest work.

In all, we received almost 1,300 submissions, most of them containing two poems each, for a total of nearly 2,500 poems. Five dedicated readers blindly ranked these submissions, sending 126 poems to this year's editor, Mark Strand, who selected the final fifty. Those five readers—Joe Chapman, David Clark, Julia Hansen, Terence Huber, and Paul Legault—deserve special thanks. All of them are practicing poets, and like prior readers, they worked hard to include not only poems they liked, but also those that they thought might interest someone with different tastes.

That last point—that we work hard to include a variety of poems and styles—is worth addressing because it begs a question we're often asked at *Best New Poets:* "What kind of poem are you looking for?" Answering that question is like trying to carry water in your hands. You can manage a few steps . . . and then it all falls away. At *Best New Poets,* our reading pool changes every year, each group different, their individual tastes varied. And while, in a perfect world, every poem submitted to *Best New Poets* would get hours of consideration by multiple readers, the reality of distilling thousands of poems to only fifty dictates an evaluation time of minutes, and often by one or two people.

But writers still ask, "Okay, but really, what do you want in a poem?"

Our standard answer is "Read past editions," from which writers will glean no more than that we generally shy away from pure L=A=N=G=U=A=G=E poetry and we don't often publish (but have published) rhyming, metered verse. Which puts us about where most every contemporary literary magazine lives. So, I'll try to be more specific, though with an ulterior motive. I'll answer, "Read our past editions— and take a good look at George Garrett's work."

George Garrett passed away this summer and, for those of us fortunate enough to have known him, it is hard to live a day when he does not come to mind. George's publications are too many to enumerate here in detail, but they range from historical fiction (*Death of the Fox* and the rest of his Elizabethan Trilogy) to biography and literary criticism, and most important to this introduction, a long, long list of poems and books of poetry (*Days of Our Lives Lie in Fragments* from LSU Press is a good place to start reading). George was a sort of literary chameleon, trying on many genres and literary forms over his career, but poetry was a lifelong passion. Yet George always balanced that inward passion with an immense kindness and generosity toward other writers. He was an early believer in this poetry series, for example, serving as the first guest editor when I could offer no pay and *Best New Poets* was utterly untested.

But I want to focus on George's work, and the way he approached it. Year after year, George wrote poems because he felt compelled to, because he loved the play of language on the tongue. And he had an uncanny ability to make his lines, his deceptively simple verse, sing. Take for example, the short poem "Postcards":

One of these times very soon
I will have and hold a day
blank as a new pillowcase
or a field of fresh snow.
And then and there once again
I will lay down my head, I will
make angels in the wet snow.
I will write words   words   words,
as you do, and will sign my name,
naming my new poems like children,
calling them home from the dark.

In "Postcards," we're only looking at three sentences, eleven lines, and yet their impact is so immediate, so complete. There is no fooling around. George often wrote his poetry to be read aloud and frequently used an almost conversational tone because he knew a live audience wasn't going to be able to go back and re-scan his lines for some obfuscated meaning. This was his own aesthetic choice, and not one that every poet will want to, or should, follow. But it's not a bad model when sending work to a book like this one. When your poem is one submission among thousands, it better have real impact on a first read.

Another characteristic of George's poetry is its frequent use of humor. On my way home from work the other day, I was sitting on the bus reading a few of George's poems—and laughing. There's this wicked snippet from a series of short poems titled "Flashcards":

To a Certain Critic

Walking in the woods, you turn over a rotten log.
Out from under crawls something very snotlike and pale.
If it could open its mouth and talk good English,
you'd know exactly what you sound like to me.

The other bus riders must have thought me touched, crazy: here's some strange guy reading poetry (for only strange people read poetry these days, stranger still on a bus) and laughing. But George gave me that permission, forced that laugher upon me as he addressed all the vagaries of the world we live in. His work reminds every poet that humor is never off limits. Here at *Best New Poets,* as we face thousands of manuscripts and read a dozen consecutive poems on death, cancer, and incest, there is something oddly refreshing about a poem that makes us smile.

Yet as humorous as George's work can be, it is also often bold, fearless. A boxer in his youth, George would sometimes tell young writers that the basic problem with landing a punch was that you had to risk getting close enough for the other guy to hit back. Poetry, too, requires risks. Read George's poem "Some Enormous Surprises" and try to imagine yourself writing about Adolf Hitler as a small boy—and getting away with it. But George does, in part, because that poem also addresses his deep Christian faith and the impossibility of ever reconciling that faith with what our world has to offer. No, please, for *Best New Poets 2009,* do not submit dozens of religious poems. That's not the point I'm making. What I'm saying is that George did not shy away from subjects that would scare off many poets, whether his poem was deadly serious or riddled with irony.

One last example from George's work that shows some of the magic I'm talking about:

Luck's Shining Child

Because I am broke again
I have the soles of my shoes repaired
one at a time.

From now on one will always be
fat and slick with new leather
while his sad twin,

lean and thin as a fallen leaf,
will hug a large hole like a wound.
When it rains

one sock and one foot get wet.
When I cross the gravel parking lot
one foot winces

and I have to hop along on the other.
my students believe I am trying
to prove something.

They think I'm being a symbol of
dichotomy, duality, double-dealing,
yin and yang.

I am hopping because it hurts.
Because there is a hole in my shoe.
Because I feel poor for keeps.

What I am trying not to do
is imagine how it will be in my coffin,
heels down, soles up,

all rouged and grinning above my polished shoes,
one or the other a respectable brother
and one or the other

that wild prodigal whom I love
as much or more than his sleek companion,
luck's shining child.

After a poem like that, what else is there to say? Not much, except, rest in peace, George, the work lives on.

And for those of you thinking about reading a little more of George Garrett's poetry or prose, how lucky you are. How wonderful it will be to watch someone accomplish more in a few pages than many of us manage over a lifetime of writing. It *is* magic, watching George at work, and how lucky all of us are when we read it again and again and again.

—Jeb Livingood
University of Virginia

Landon Godfrey

Second-Skin Rhinestone-Spangled Nude Soufflé Chiffon Gown

Tonight I will be sewn into it.

Tonight Kenneth will sweep my white-blonde bouffant into a side flip.

Tonight I will clutch at my milky mink wrap like a baby kangaroo climbing
pouch-ward.

Tonight I will flirt. But I will not make jokes like *Now Napoleon knows what
Bonaparte really means* or pun *taupe* & *topos* or try to rhyme them with *top hat*
because I believe no one can.

Tonight a million flash bulbs will Morse Code my one human wish.

Tonight this gown will draw fingertips towards my body like a starving galaxy
devouring dark matter. The fingers of the men. The men.

Tonight I will whisper, *Je ne comprends rien, Sugar Pie,* and my left-cheek mole will
answer, *We're almost there.*

—*Nominated by* The Southeast Review

Anna Journey

Adorable Siren, Do You Love the Damned?

—Baudelaire

The devil pries open my red hibiscus, like skirts. On the crack
        corner those transvestite hookers won't quit
competing with my garden's

barbed and carnal tongues. The bitch
        scent of the silver

and pink-clawed possum in heat—all rhubarb-breath and unbelievable
        udder—is sharp as fuchsia

spokes of my oleander. I could put
        my eye out looking. I could run with knives. Outside the brine

of B.O. tangles with perfume—bodies that snag
        men like my singing

can't. This song won't dress up, won't wear black
        patent leather, won't even shave

its five o'clock shadow—lazy sliver
       slumming the telltale animal. What song, devil, is best
sung from my balcony

in my birthday suit, by my heartleaf nightshade's
       liquory patina? I'm drunk,
though I won't wear heels, honey, or I'd fall

for anyone. I'd fall devil
       over heels over edge over oleander
over open mouth

over birthmark over forked
       tongue over forked tongue
that turns on mine.

—Nominated by the University of Houston

Aby Kaupang

It takes a pillage to sing a Strom song:

A village to make a nation
gross. The National Product is gross.

Strom looks at it
from both sides—two sides—now
from X's and O's and still
somehow it's personal
illusions Strom recalls.

Style? Still Strom.   Mael___.
Whoa. Down now boy.

There's a pony in Strom,
a stallion among us.

Who can know love at all?

Strom days are roses:

We are burying Strom

it's a way of keeping the flesh
at bay
        Stromland security

a baby cries herself out
we acquire a bridge   singe
a bridge   we are   older
no rest no peas   in the queue

        Listen to the Thurmond on the mount

he says to her back *should we*
get tattoos you and   to the door
I together?

        Stromming my heart with her fingers

she would throw rugs

        Strom diddy Strom
        diddy Strom {3x}

another round of goat songs

Alone, amid the fires:

smoke and mirrors/
mirrors and smoke

and the camp songs and the ponderosas

my love's rosy lips
afloat in the brine

thin Strom wonders at Libra imbalanced in the skies.

Strom hopes (he's a feathery thing):

Strom needs everyday
everyday in _____ to be a good day

for a deal. *Ours:*
the stray and the struth and the slight.

A new deal.

He who buys into segregation buys
Modernity:
        the front porch tazer
        the forehead tent
        the nano comfort

Nobody knows it but Thurmond's so sad.

The beginning of love, he mused,
is a feeding tube on the sly.

He fingers a name in the soot.

—*Nominated by Colorado State University*

Tracey Knapp

Difficulties

I fell asleep in the grocery line while
waiting to buy you a ham. I was waiting
for the right moment to tell you.
I told you about my first time in
Cincinnati, the man on the bus
who smelled of formaldehyde.
I can still feel his wool jacket
scratching against my bare arm.
I can barely feel my fingers.
It's so cold that the whiskers
on my dog look like icicles. We
are walking towards the sun's last
attempt. The snow is stacked so high
but my dog begins digging like there's
an enormous flank of steak beneath,
and what does he pull up but his old
squeaky whale! We hadn't seen it since
summer. It's been a difficult winter.
It's been difficult to smoke pot
with my accountant. He tells me
it's not the sixties, and it's not the first

time I've heard that. The first time I heard
about your sick cat, I tried to call but
I heard you were turning yourself
into a grain of sand. I have turned
you into a grain of sand.
This is the first time I can honestly
say that. The first glass of wine
was followed by the next and now
it's the first Monday at this new
desk, the first Monday I haven't spent
the evening loathing my thighs
over a glass of wine. Where there's
self-loathing, there's yourself,
and then the one bright thing
underneath that makes life
worth digging for.

—*Open Competition*

Darren Morris

Counting Down the Night

Ten boughs for the darling who longs for the lizard-faced boy.
Ten songs for his sick mother. Ten lashes on the ogre's back for carrying
the hay barn across the river, but ten kindnesses if he should drown.
Four eggs and a loaf of rye bread make the poor family's dinner tonight,
which makes the six of them sleep, even the father under the night's long feather,
be it twill of winter, uncompromising and bare, or the promise
of nothing in the hours of their next hunger. Praise the daughter twice,
her tendril-bone, praise her anxiety, her rattling tooth of wind,
her flakes of skin. If you were to die right now. If you were to be no more,
it would be no more than the smallest of these. To go wordlessly in sleep.
To go without a father, a mother, a simple dog who whimpers; these
who would be no more. It is that vacuum of disappearance. That final,
unforgivable seal. The sheep over the fence. The bloody wool caught in the barb.
The bleating of the little one lost, as they pound on, relentlessly. The puma
from which they run. The night's cliff just beyond their knowing. It is this
finality that allows us to stretch out now. Way out there. Where it all could
just melt away. Where we may pluck them from the floe, find each clue,
and shear. Make way. Safely to the barn. When I have wet sheep warming
in their stalls, all will be quiet, but for the little one lost. And if ever
the lantern tips, the ogre will carry the burning barn off to the river to drown.

—*Nominated by* Memorius: A Journal of New Verse and Fiction

Christopher Louvet

Brackish Rhapsody

I.

Didn't I meet you
once, in Stockholm,

didn't you syndrome
or syndicate terror

into me, your ostrich,
your mendicant,

didn't I wake up
with your constellation

inscribed on my thighs,
my fingerprints?

Or was it Stendhalian?
Because ill-timed coins,

spent to empty bottles,
delivered me to theater

in the armor, protective
as a turned-out pocket,

of the Order of Love
that Knows No Latitudes.

II.

Words you never
pronounced to learn

correctly cough
my ribcage

and ulcer my veins
like a yolk

bordering its spurning
in the skillet

on a perfect
Sunday morning

as a papier-mâché,
full-frontal hangover

begins from behind
and eggs its way

off the bed, to the sofa
to the floor,

where all the fun is,
where our language

doesn't have a gun or
any rules to recognize.

III.

Our grammar,
especially

the soft, prolonged *ahs*
like the long, slow slough

of hurricane hours,
and the sharper, shorter *ohs*

that crack like rain
on the windowpanes,

the windy shudders
in our conjunctions!

—*Open Competition*

Alexandra Teague

Adjectives of Order

That summer, she had a student who was obsessed
with the order of adjectives. A soldier in the South
Vietnamese army, he had been taken prisoner when

Saigon fell. He wanted to know why the order
could not be altered. The sweltering city streets shook
with rockets and helicopters. The city sweltering

streets. On the dusty brown field of the chalkboard,
she wrote: *The mother took warm homemade bread
from the oven. City* is essential to *streets* as *homemade*

is essential to *bread*. He copied this down, but
he wanted to know if his brothers were *lost* before
older, if he worked security at a twenty-story modern

downtown bank or downtown twenty-story modern.
When he first arrived, he did not know enough English
to order a sandwich. He asked her to explain each part

of *Lovely big rectangular old red English Catholic
leather Bible*. Evaluation before size. Age before color.
Nationality before religion. Time before length. Adding

and, one could determine if two adjectives were equal.
After Saigon fell, he had survived nine long years
of torture. Nine *and* long. He knew no other way to say this.

—*Open Competition*

Cynthia Lowen

Notes from the Target Committee

I. Tokyo

> *Tokyo is a possibility, but it is now practically all bombed and*
> *burned out...*
> —The Target Committee

here, white shadow of Meiji Street
here, white shadow of what was formerly called
the center metastasizing up the vein

of the Onagi River: the reconnaissance photos return
x-rays of a doomed lung
from 1,500 feet

white heads of cauliflower
blooming from the open cavity
tissue aggregating tissue

tumors of white fire against the black
negative—invasive vegetable,
breaking off, re-rooting

in the liver, the brain, Yokohama,
Nagoya, island of terminal
shadows, rifled, run through

the CAT for one unspoiled
organ over which a different shadow
might fall

II. Kyoto

> *I don't want Kyoto bombed.*
> —Secretary of War Henry L. Stimson

Breaking the spirit
is not ruining

        completely

but preserving a temple

to return to:
model on which the rubble

will be compelled again
towards sky

not as temples
but proof

defeat
is only reiterated

by second incarnations.

The spirit breaks
with the knowledge

of the choice—

that the monuments
paving the infinite dirt road
to enlightenment

were admired—

match in one hand
prayer in the other.

III. Hiroshima

That no passing cloud
intervened. And the earth did not quake

to say, *enough*.

That maggots tunneled through dirt
knowing not hunger but purpose.

And crows circled above knowing flesh is servant
to hunger and purpose.

That blood
was iron in the rock.

And the skin would be pricked
to prove this.

That each thistle was a scythe
cutting the thread to this world.

That this world was the thread
in the first place.

That thirst. That earthly bodies
succumb to. And the sun was a fever

not to be taken personally. And the thistle

was not accountable
for the thorn's perversion.

That the spirit collected dirt
beneath its fingernails.

That the spirit appealed to the moon's
blank face, feeling no sense

of communion.

And the crowd
cheered. And the crowd

found excuse
for their ordinary failures

seeing it was not
an empire.

That exhaustion. Which earthly bodies
admit to.

And women wept into their scarves
to later meet a shadow there.

Let pity be exercised

on the that which has
no use for it.

Let the scythe rest
at the mountain of its harvest.

May maggots discover their purpose.

May the passing clouds
carry

the earthly body
away.

Let its absence be mistaken
for forgiveness

when later the crowd
comes looking.

IV. Nagasaki

> *At Nagasaki there was a thick overcast...then,*
> *at the last moment a hole in the clouds*
> *appeared, permitting visual bombing.*
> —General Leslie R. Groves

Sometimes I hate you
for not stopping me
from hurting you

says the hurricane
inside the eye

where dandelions momentarily display
perfect white afros.

On the Doppler
a red cornea haloes
the steel blue iris

and the weatherman warns

suspect any day shaped
like a donut

where only the hole
is habitable.

When the hurricane wants to believe itself
it says

I'm better
now

as if just by saying so
it might dissipate

into a front
that passed last week.

Inside the eye
tattoos are not storms
by other women's names

but apologies
the short memory accepts
because it has to.

On the lawn
dandelions hold their heads
like glasses on a tray

and the pinhole of sky
is wide as the picture

the mind takes
of a place it wants to remember.

Sometimes I think
we could live
like this

forever says the hurricane
reaching out
two fingers of wind

to pluck the first white seed.

—*Nominated by the Fine Arts Work Center in Provincetown*

Drew Blanchard

Watching Fire

The blaze of maple's orange and sumac's red
has fallen away, and gingko's golden fans
are all that remain. The earth is ashy now
with leaves, a carpet of crackling death, and yet
I love the feel of life before we retreat
for winter, to breathe the same air again and again.
Last week my neighbor's wife walked out on him,
a note left on the bed read sadness and pain.
I know this because he and a fifth
of Johnny Walker didn't go home until
my kitchen windows turned from black to gray
and pink—an autumn sun our final call.
The next day, raking leaves, I heard a crash
from Jerry's house, and then his sweaty head
poked out the back door. Looking wildly around
he dragged, banging and clanking, a bedframe
into the middle of his lawn. Smiling, he walked
back inside. A minute later he returned,
the mattress cut in two; he tossed the pieces
on the broken frame. After a few hours,
a sculpture of shoes and books,

of clothes and kitchen utensils, amassed
in Jerry's backyard.

                When my parents divorced
I didn't see such passion screaming from them.
I was ten, the same year Father said "it's time,"
my brother and I finally old enough
to help him chop and gather wood. We scoured
ravines behind our house and down to Trout
Creek in search of fallen oaks and elms.
Father cut hundred-year-old trees into wedges
small enough to chop. Small pieces of dust
and chips clung to his beard and clothes,
cloaking him in what he was dismantling.
The strangest thing I recall the year Mother left,
was that Father, who never wasted the good oak,
our fuel for the stove, built a fire that burned
late into the dark of an autumn night.

—Nominated by the University of Wisconsin-Milwaukee

Lisa Ottiger

Rainlight

He came upon them dancing.
He was late because it had started to rain
and he had taken shelter under an awning
to wait it out. The rain had started out
as a light mist, droplets so fine
that they condensed on his jacket
without his noticing until it began
to rain harder and he realized he was already
wet through, and soon his sketchpad would
be as well and his hair was dripping down
his collar because, of course, he had no hat.
When he had arrived in Paris to study art,
the very atmosphere had unnerved him.
The light in France was different, soft and watery,
it seemed to be filtered through a veil
so that the world was always slightly out-of-focus,
not altogether tangible. He too had felt
not altogether tangible in this wavering landscape.
He had expected to feel a sense of belonging
when he arrived, but instead he felt invisible.
There was no one here who knew him,

when all his life his name and his family
had been a thing to be considered,
they had a form and a weight like holding
a stone in your hand. The French his father
had taught him was out of date, his pronunciation
full of hard, foreign syllables, not like the slithering
rush of language that Parisians spoke,
and they looked so pale and strange, their skin
a greenish-white that was nothing like his own.
Sometimes he felt that he was only held in this place
by the weight of his clothes. In cafes,
on the sidewalks, at the theatre,
they stared at him and asked him
what he was, and listed the possibilities:
Italian, Algerian, Chinese, Japanese, Indian?
No one believed he was French,
so he told them he was a Spaniard
and that they could pretend to believe.
The rain had slowed and he left
his dry harbour and arrived
at 127 Boulevard Sant-Germain quite out of breath.
It was a large, white, solid house,
looking rather as he imagined
the people who lived there would look.
The skinny maid who opened the door
looked him over disapprovingly before
letting him into the front hall and taking
his wet coat. The hallway was dark
and he had sensed the maid was impatient,
but Miguel took the time to look into the gilt mirror

hanging on the wall and straighten his hair to annoy her.
The maid had watched him part his hair
and smooth it into place. Something was not right
about him, she had thought, but she could not say what.
She had been told to expect an artist and here
was a hatless young man with a sketchpad—
of course an artist but his clothes were not artistic—
he looked like a banker in his black suit.
He was not very tall but solidly built, and his face,
she thought there might be something foreign
about his face—perhaps he was a Jew?
Miguel had gathered up his things when he was satisfied
and she showed him to the sitting room
where he came upon them dancing,
Patrice and his sister practicing a turn around an armchair,
and Miguel saw the girl drop her slipper
then step back into it, a dainty little trick
designed to show off her pretty dancing
and her prettier ankles to any who might care to look.
Inès leaned against her brother to catch her breath.
She was a beauty, Miguel saw—
she was sallow and there were dark circles
under her eyes, but it didn't matter.
She returned his gaze, unblinking,
and he recognized her. In his former life
he had seen women like her;
but they were wearing *piña* blouses
that did not cover so much as dapple their skin,
their hair was scented with ylang-ylang
and pinned with tortoise-shell combs,

and they had driven in open victorias
by the bay in the hour before sunset and as the wind
drifted off the water they had concealed
their faces behind undulating lace fans,
lowering their lashes over their brilliant black eyes
in a sign language he did not know.

—*Open Competition*

Steve Kistulentz

The David Lee Roth Fuck Poem with Language Taken from
Van Halen I, 1984, *and The First Letter of the Apostle Paul*
To the Church at Corinth

What you are expecting is a familiar riff on the theme
of girls and cars, where Laurel Canyon rings with big beast reverb
and in the top-down weather, the freeways clog with dinosaur
machines all pointed towards the water gone green,
sky lighting up the boulevard, Pacific Ocean blue poured on gasoline.

It's a new leather jacket and stiletto boots and four girls
from high school, too young but still cute, pink high tops and hula hoops
in the back of Daddy's Cadillac, 455 cubic inches of open throat,
the sound a boy makes when he imitates *hot shoes*
burning down the avenue. I pass and I leer and they give me

the universal salute, extended middle finger, even the driver,
both hands off the wheel. We orbit the light, circle the block and I tell them
the most honest thing I know: *the way of love is the highway,*
and in your malice you are still children. I was sent to give
sparkling advice in strange tongues, though my tongue should cease.

Because all you have to do is slide down out of the
hillsides and see the runaways staggering up Sepulveda, begging quarters
for the RTD. Hollywood is the gaping maw of an insatiable clown which
devours everything it sees, indiscriminate in its appetites,
and soon you girls will be dancing seven sets a night, three songs a set,

garbed in the sacramental costumes of sexy librarians
and or Catholic school nurses, whatever. We *ain't talking 'bout love*,
but rather the feel of velvet cream dollars tucked into a saggy garter,
the soundtrack reminders to take care of your bartender,
your waitress, for every dancer down to just her fishnets to Windex

mirror and pole at the end of each three song set,
house rules, and be sure to tip out the busboys who so deliriously vow to
become men who drive convertibles with white vinyl interiors and festoon
the rearview with dice and a piña colada-scented freshener.
It is as if California causes blindness, an inability to see the future.

So let me tell you how it is going to be: once the
evening is gas-filled for ten dollars a tank, everybody who wants some
can park at Carl's Junior and walk to curbside, where a ponytailed girl
waits only for someone willing to listen to the tribulations
of being fourteen, to sing her a love song of how the six-dollar burger

once only cost three, and hope alternately meant the sound
of Stratocasters or glass-pack mufflers, or even the big beat of bass drum,
and if I speak in the tongues of men I am only a clanging cymbal
of warnings, part known, part obvious. There's always
a Doctor Feelgood paying off cops in the back of Winchell's Donuts,

and there's always a guy waiting out back with a business card,
one that says *producer* but who actually owns the Carl's Junior franchise
down the block and he says things like: come run away with me,
because that is what a girl must learn to do when she casts aside
her Topeka past. Come run away with me for a six-dollar burger

laden with any condiment you desire. And me, Diamond Dave,
I am a messenger here with this fair warning. That man, what he desires
is to *reach down between his legs and ease the seat back*, and he'll tell you
leave the shoes on. Stand firm. Let nothing move you.
I'll tell him myself: *don't you know she's coming home with me?*

—*Open Competition*

Keith Ekiss

Pima Road Notebook (II)

Always the abandoned mattress springs in the arroyo.
And sunlight dusting tattered afternoon curtains.
Down street, the boy who stuttered but could sing.
No one she could talk to like she wanted to talk.
I should've been her lovely girl.
My father said he made something from nothing, like sons.
Brothers were other animals.
Javalina bristled for water outside my sleep.
Coyotes gathered and chattered in guttural moans.
All night she thought the howls were only dogs.
My body's better use, casting a shadow for a quail.
I watched the tame hawk return to its hooded wrist.
She dropped me off for school at Cherokee Elementary.
Heat pulsing in my temple and sweat.
I found a nest of rabbits hidden in the cholla.
The young are born helpless, naked, and blind.

—*Nominated by* Blackbird

Heidi Johannesen Poon

Global Warming

The candle lit
Starts taking off
With utter faith

Its old violet sweater
Into the sink.
And now there's wax

In the elbow of drain—
To be around in the days
And nights to come

Where laughter won't expand
Is to understand
The landlord doesn't need this.

*

The chair isn't a fool
When it rocks on the porch
In the wind. The fool's inside.

Bit by bit, the world divides.
The storm outside
Will always seem

Too light to speak of.
The screen door slams—
The brain thinks in the dark.

The human heart so made
To be working, so that's how
It's finally resting,

Over these wide newbearing fields
Where all the chairs have been cleared
(the audience near)

And the final version grows.

—Open Competition

Michael Bazzett

Clouds and Mountains

the alpine meadows were arid
the high air dry in spite of snowmelt
the lakes vivid jade and cerulean blue
the smell of sage and scrub spruce dusting
the hard rim of everything after a day
of climbing higher than the mountain

goats who shed their winter coats in
woolly shreds on every twisted branch
near camp they drummed across the rocks
the sodden meadow tufts to lick our
piss clean from blackened boulders with even
blacker tongues murmuring *salt! here is salt!*

we sat after all that climbing in the shallow
hollow of our camp the ravine not a ravine
but a ditch and braided with goat paths
and we watched the clouds come low
and hairy sprawling over the ridge rising
from froze-to-death plateau to settle on

the saddle slung between high ridge and
granite peak and blue those clouds are
blue we said aloud as we sat and looked
up at the dark mountain rising into the mist
the clouds curled heavy and fluid
as a satisfied cat around the broken

granite that sometimes clattered down
into talus and scree and the boulder fields
rimming avalanche lake where we sat
wrapped in every layer we'd brought as it
darkened and became harder to tell
what was cloud and what was mountain

we pointed toward where the constellations
would have been and lapsed into a silence
until the sound of rock sliding and cracking
open on other rock cut through the dark
and we looked toward the clatter to see
sparks slicing through the fallen night

raining from rockslide bright as white
knives and for one slipping down moment
the only clear thing in the entire world was
light shot out from that unstoppable falling.

—Open Competition

Paul Longo

Shiny Shiny

The idea of an adaptive path
was "just an idea"
stemmed from motions
we should be ourselves
be Authentic have many
balls & drop them
through the model
without them realizing
we are doing diagnostic
on them, building
and maintaining a safe
successful nuclear pharmacy
requires a wide variety of services: the ideal
system is precise, sensitive, offers immediate
adjustment and control—thank god
it's a one-off, the radium fog's so thick
we almost see the sun
we like the shiny shiny
smart salesman: he has a customer
for life now, a body to wrap around
the framework and poke and prod

our dense web of the plausible
filling us with feelings of
insane loyalty is pure
marketing mouthwash
we lost our nerve we fell
silent no one queued
to see the strategy or develop
a "well place" as a product
of god's intent, replacing something
menacing with practically pretty
as in gets-things-done
the auto intelligence of pretty
just now entering its deadliest phase.

—*Open Competition*

Adam Day

Hiding Again in London

        The streets, black with rain and stately-lit, I walk
past the British Museum to University College,
      where the Socialist Workers Party is screening *Land and Freedom*.
I am hiding in the audience, looking
         for beautiful women—confusing jargon: class intercourse,

        sexual warfare—aware of the probability
of defeat. What, in the end, can we know
      of each other? I fell in love with Marx
several years before, though, in life, he despised the lower classes—
        as we despise ourselves—making him one of us.

        How could he not be: chronically writing to Engels
for 10 pounds here, 20 pounds there; boils, jaundice, grippe;
      three children dead of poverty; bread and potatoes for days;
and not an unbroken piece of furniture in the house. After
        the Anarchists and Communists lose to Franco the lights

come up, pints are served in the student annex,
where I talk with two Argentine friends about anything
      but politics or exile, the *añoranza*: soccer mostly, and the beautifully pale
English girl across the room, Elizabeth, who is looking
      at me, and away, and back again. Outside—she tells me

      about her professor parents, her home in Sussex
where sweet William pins itself to the slats of the front porch,
      and she walks out to horse-stables in the morning
in jodhpurs and a tank-top. Then, scattershot
      of car horns—a hand suddenly unpocketed, the hairs

      on our arms touching—even at night, the riot
of poppies in spring. Beside our confused feet
      a lung-sore bum with his *Guardian* tent and cardboard mat
is sleeping, as I push her breasts up, beneath her sweater.
      Months like this passed before I left for Stockholm

      carrying that nameless thing that we've always known
without having learned, more alive for it's anonymity:
      that we'll lose, that we're history-haunted, that speaking
into silence our gods, parent-ghosts, and lovers
      may not hear us. Still, call him. Awkwardly call this man,

      "Bear," of all things, as his family did, through hob
and tobacco smoke—just up from bed, he's still sitting
      in his study on the Isle of Wight, where he has put
his head down—blue capillaries under skin
      as thin as rice paper—with the hard-focused eyes

of a man one week at the bottom of a lake—
and what is the vocabulary for that, how
can words deliver love—I say it is raining
over the mountains and mean I am rolling onto my side
to fall asleep next to you.

—Nominated by The Antioch Review

Angie Mazakis

RFI (Request for Information)

Introduction

Because I am anxious that provocative and
meaningful coincidence is possible and might
elude me,

I am requesting the following information.

Background

As a child, desperate for resolution, I created
explanations. For every movie, my own *dues ex machina*
played in my mind, like a countermelody to the plot,
for the lovers or friends kept apart in the end
by dueling families, by betrayal or infidelity, or
most tragically—by some unromantic interference.
After the credits rolled, I allowed them to
sneak out of the house, send penitent flowers, awake
from death and dreams. And all the unresolved difficulties
that the writers left wavering at the end of the story,

were just accidents. Just unavoidable accidents which
were actually ironic and humorous
when you untangled the complications.

Objectives

I need better associations and connectors.

I would like to be able to categorize specific
circumstances as either meaningful or arbitrary.

All I want is for things to be explained.

Statement of Need

> ▶ A list of the four people on earth who look
> most like me

(My name called out loud in a place I have
never been, over and over, with no answer.)

> ▶ A list of unique utterances or thoughts of consecutive
> words which I have spoken or thought, which
> were spoken verbatim by someone else without my
> knowledge on any occasion, unique enough
> for the repetition to be significant.

(A narcoleptic in Louisiana saying, almost defensively,
without ever having heard of Descartes,

There are no certain indications by which we may distinguish
wakefulness from sleep, that I am lost in astonishment.)

> ▶ A list of unique utterances of consecutive words
> spoken by me and someone else at the exact moment,
> unknown to each of us.

(In our separate childhoods, Emily in Ohio and
me in Indiana, among our repeated quoting of the
line, *I'm tired of going up the down staircase,*
on any occasion, coinciding.

A stranger on a train in Topeka as I am on an airplane
over Seattle in February thinking synchronously,
The sun on the daffodils outside the bay window...)

> ▶ A diagram which marks the lineage of all those, living
> or otherwise, who have come within two degrees of
> separation from me, including in the first degree,
> beyond acquaintances, encounters with strangers
> whom I would remember if generously reminded.

(The little girl in Venezuela, singing in the kitchen.
The Miss America contestant who sat next to me
on an airplane who kept asking for more chocolate
and spoke of the pageant with embarrassment.
The anonymous boy in the store in South Bend.
His brothers or sisters. Any of their faces
in this picture of a crowd in a Sociology book I'm leafing through.)

▶ A spreadsheet of sums that reflect the frequency
of my recalling the repetition of something arbitrary,
significant to me only in its repetition.

(Some obscure catalogue, which you've seen twice
in other people's houses. Once in Canada.

The three story tudor-style house on Interstate 69
somewhere after Muncie, Indiana, a transgression
on the countryside, which I've passed four times, its
incongruous cross gables darkened by night, and which
appears in my thoughts, when I feel apprehensive.)

▶ A mailing list, with phone numbers, of all the people
on earth, according to empirical evidence and under
varying circumstances, with whom I would sustain
the most meaningful, familiar, satiating affinity with
enough imperfection to be complicated.

(I am taking my change from one of them now, at the grocery
store, in the only interaction we'll ever have. Would my
grandmother in South Bend, Indiana have been included
on this list? She died when I was five, before I could ever
ask her about our last day alone together, shopping for summer
clothes. Did she hear the music I heard, and had the melodies
in our minds been played out loud, would the chords have
layered into counterpoint, as the rain hurried us home?)

▶ Flash cards corresponding to everyone I will ever meet
revealing the ways I will underestimate how they matter.

(The little boy in the store in South Bend whose mom
and siblings drifted to an abstracted part of my memory,
while he remained by himself, near me and my
grandmother, in the brief moment that he was an
anonymous boy who I would have forgotten forever.

The woman in the same store who looked just like
Suzanne Somers, which made her seem comically
harmless, her perfect blonde hair reaching her waist when
she leaned over to ask the boy his name, the counter-
melody pacifying my mind and negotiating that she was
his ironic and theatrical aunt playing a game they knew.

The cashier to whom the blonde woman said,
glibly, "He always does this," to deflate the boy's
desperate crying and protest, as she pulled the boy out
the front door, letting the disproportion into the store—
the permanent absence which surrounded
whatever department to where his mother had wandered.

And her, the mother, resurfacing slowly to the front of the
store, her voice calling out his name in equidistant measure,
[while another mother in Florida called out a different name
concurrently, or in exact syncopation, or in a slower, sadder
rhythm fifteen years earlier], the metronome of her voice
recalling for me the cross gables, black narrow windows,
and sloping roof, rising as recollection for the first time.)

—Open Competition

S.E. Smith

Bedroom Community

We met in the most interesting place in America
which, it turns out, is any place that has a corner store.
All those black pills at the counter, bagged in twos,
like Snow White's eyes in "Snow White: the Comic Book."
I had a theory about oil and wine emulsions re:
the perfect glaze but was not ready to share it. And he said,
You look like the kind of girl who has a cat. And I said,
Who doesn't? All that steady lamplight turning
the sidewalk into snow. The fountain in his residential
area had been shut down until spring, so we walked
through a series of gates and enclosures to find another
fountain. There we composed letters to *American Bungalow*
magazine. His began, "Bungalow owners will rejoice to find
that memory is not a room, it is a bungalow." Mine began,
"I am writing in response to your September article
on unconventional salt and pepper shakers, which, in my
estimation, can only be considered 'unconventional'
if they are filled with something other than salt or pepper."
All that sand and graphite on the dinner, turning our teeth
into dingy pearls. We praised the fountain because it was full
of feeling but ultimately transparent. We praised the electric
chandelier: shorthand for "flame." Think of a transistor

as a bucket full of invisible water, he said, and I said
why not invisible wine, or some kind of oil and wine emulsion?
It's easy once you get the hang of it. It's only cold because
of all this wind howling from its pulpit on the beach.
If god wanted us to be strangers, why would he place us
next to each other in the movie theater and make us think
our knees are touching? Looking at Anita Ekberg's breasts,
we can see the future. It is soft, pink, and frolics in a fountain
where the sea gods bathe their weary feet.

—Open Competition

Charlotte Savidge

Mattress Shopping

I'm going mattress shopping with my ex-boyfriend Jack,
and we're crossing Queens Boulevard,
known to the locals as the highway of death,
so Jack crosses himself melodramatically
before stooping to throw me over his shoulder
and fake launch us into the traffic,
exhibiting the characteristic carefree physicality
that both charms and unsettles me,
as I was raised with a pat on the back
in place of a hug, but then
he sets me down, takes my hand,
and we bolt across before the light turns green.
Arriving safely in front of a Sleepy's,
we enter the gleaming glass-enclosed mattress oasis
in the midst of rundown industrial Queens
and are immediately greeted by a beaming saleswoman

who promptly refers us to the on-sale circulars
and a black contraption at the end of the showroom
that will measure the pressure points in Jack's lumbar region,
and as he's complained of lower back pain—

the result most likely of sharing the couch
with his seventeen-pound cat—I suggest
he give it a whirl, so Jack lies down
and the saleswoman inputs his info—
Height? Weight? Sleeping partner, yes or no?
and I can just tell Jack's thinking, Should the cat count?—
when the machine spits out a list of brands he should try,
and as we move from Sealy Posturpedic
to Miralux Rapture Pillow Top,

the saleswoman—who's keeping a respectable distance
despite the fact we're the only ones in the place
and she's probably just aching to offer someone else
a ride on the leatherette lumbar bed—
peruses Jack's sleep pattern form
and says, *Hey, you forgot your wife,*
to which he replies, *She's not my wife,*
she's just a friend. And the saleslady, a woman who
most likely has had her own share of he's-just-a-friends,
raises an eyebrow, as Jack pats the open space beside him,
noting there'll be room for both me and the cat.

And as I'm lying there on the Serta Perfect Sleeper,
eyes closed, imagining it in Jack's bedroom,
I suddenly remember my best friend Scott—
whom I'd known since high school and who
dropped out of Columbia to become a bike messenger
and live in a squat and whose
lack of concern for basic social graces
led him to say things like, *how about if I*

go to you for conversation and
Silvana for sex, which, while brutal
always assured me I knew where I stood, and
that alone was refreshing and kind of
comforting actually—and I'm thinking of
how the summer before Scott died
we decided to walk the full length of Manhattan,
a true urbanite's odyssey—
But we can't walk on Broadway—

and as the route not the timeframe was the only restriction
we stopped at V&T's Pizza on 110th,
the center of the Earth as far as Scott was concerned
since they served the world's only *orgiastic* eggplant pie.
And it's no wonder I'm thinking of Scott
while testing out mattresses for my not-husband Jack,
as it was during that halfway point break
on our epic trek from Battery Park to the Bronx
that Scott leaned in toward me, across the pizza pan—
empty except for a few stray pieces of anchovy
that must have looked to the chef like slivers of eggplant—
as if to bestow a we've-come-this-far kiss,
and said, *Don't ever let me marry you—*

and sometimes I still wonder
what would have happened
if Scott had survived the freak accident
that cut short his life by some forty years,
and no matter how hard I try
to keep track of the fact that I'm right here, in this moment,

in a Sleepy's in Queens, being warmed by the sun
on an exceptionally bright winter day,
while I practically float on a foam pad
with my friend Jack beside me,
deep inside
I can't help but feel cold.

—Open Competition

Eva Hooker

Before the Spring in Which the Forsythia Bloom
And She Unravels All Her Chambers, Mother Writes

I will not let my knees bow nor my hands be lifted up
she said I am

Asleep or absent in the snowy hills
following rules for order as if they were new wool

In hand in whose comparison all whites are ink
and nothing

In motion shall clarify: at your first waking, *straight frame*
Thyself, she said, and careful:

We're born naked, all the rest is drag

I put away the silk virtue being made out of shadow
not cloth and note

The peculiar
accuracy of its knife and sharps—

It puts the heart in my chest on bloody wings—

And pull up the tent pegs like the Russian olive
in its shaky winter idiom

I keep moving, employed as scrivener: what you do
And say when you are lost

Is how you are found

—*Nominated by* The Harvard Review

Kerri French

After Her Stroke, Our Family Remembers the Hurricane

Around the table, she blinks her response
to our questions and listens to the noise
the rest of us make, nodding her head
until someone forgets and pauses halfway
through the story: *Tell us what happened next.*
Through the window, this year's tobacco
is just visible behind the barn.
The room is bright and everything silent,
even the break of the crop's stalks in the wind.
Someone else picks up where the last
left off, and another interrupts to tell it
better, the afternoon losing itself to the rain
that has just set in. She turns away
from us to face the window, my uncle
visible beneath the thunder as he collects
damaged leaves. When she thinks no one
is watching, her hands rise to the neck
and I see her fingers trace the throat,
the outline where the voice once belonged.

—*Open Competition*

Marcia Popp

strike up the band

when my grandfather was fourteen he collected five dollars from everybody in his small town who could afford it sent away for twelve cornets one instruction book and twelve folders of march music from a place in chicago when they arrived in a big wooden crate he sat down taught himself to play then taught the boys and men in his town until they made a band that marched in vandalia and all around the state it wasn't easy because his father got religion at about the same time he said music was the work of the devil and threw my grandfather's cornet down the well my grandfather climbed down the well dried out the horn it played fine his father buried it in the garden my grandfather dug it up again it still played finally his father said my grandfather could just go to hell if he was that determined later when religion didn't mean that much to him anymore my great-grandfather said that is my boy up there leading the band.

—*Open Competition*

Luke Johnson

Poinsettias

Head-bowed in the impossible
posture pews at my mother's church,
I'd close my eyes and call out
the creeds and catechisms of her life,
those prayers like one of her mother's
recipes, steaming on the table
from memory. It's not much different

now, the few times I make it to service,
even when I see in the bulletin
that one of the multitude
of poinsettias at the front of the chapel
is watered in memory of my mother.
I'm probably calling on something
of that childhood, some sense
that I belong where I am,
that it's not just another gallon of gas.

Magnolias bloom at the bottom
of stained glass windows,
and I can hear the prayers of the people,

the inconsequential murmurs
and the well-articulated deaths
that the rafters swallow up
until they all sound the same,
like a memory of a time before
memories, of fresh-cut grass and supper.

—Open Competition

Jennifer Militello

Personality State: Prophet

I asked to be made in the image of the Lord,
as an ode to a god I'd forgotten.
I paled like a throat of birch.
I paled at the thought of such fast wings.

I preferred the god of beating to the god
of flightless limbs. I chipped bit by bit
at the bones of this until I had a voice to take me
by the hand. I preferred the god of fragments.

Each small animal fallen wild. What I thought
was cold cried in the night like an abandoned well.
Snow falling not far from here, the verb of
what will listen. The cold stretch of terrace

in the moon. Away where evening sings
its wet leaves clustered like flint, its font
an insomnia from which we crack, its retinas
as clock-beautiful as logic. I remembered the name

of the closeness of dark, its carriages rolling
back through time to yoke the ghosts of oxen.
I could see its cry already like a weapon at the anvil,
its stethoscope that cannot find the heart.

—*Nominated by* The Kenyon Review

Clint Frakes

Mystery Not Always Unkind

*And who am I? the man sleeping at the border asks, that in my love
dream sleep I have become the guardian of the lion?*
                                        —Robert Duncan

John Berryman where *did* you put those translations?
It's already November & I've conjured 23 oceans in my search.
I looked first under that black Minneapolis bridge,
            then wide Nebraska & its tiled stations,
                    murals of gone bison
                            & righteous soft red wheat,
    Oklahoma draped purple in July, like the time
            the cop let me and the yoga girl off with a warning
                & we ambushed the Super 8 swimming pool
            unbathed & thirsty.
Wyoming was to me just a blown PCV on hot prairie
            & we picked sage until the cavalry came,
                    patient in our dark skin.

Farewell then and now to land speculations.
They say you cannot tear a cloud in half,
            only stare it down until one of you breaks.

After I licked my lips in the crosswinds
       it was half a yellow moon that dried me,
   fresh out of the pool
       under the aching unrest of spheres.

  I am not King of the Dead,
      but rising in the ranks
           eons behind those Jains brushing the earth
   with sapling brooms
      not to accrue the assassin's weight
      in a step.

Something beautiful always emerges from underfoot:
    the smell of wet volcanic soil,
              lean yarrow;
     hummingbirds push on honeysuckle—
      & even in Detroit
   hawks dive,
     just like you,

John Berryman,
I *can* love what I can't understand, but
    it takes an ounce of grace & seasons more kind.
Let's dance then & now
    even if we are poorer than we are sad
      with fathers fallen under the plow
  & the old Appaloosa curling its lip,
    brought kicking to the final field.

                 —*Open Competition*

Seth Abramson

Nebraska

1981,
        & for three days in Nebraska
penny loafers are the talk, the 30s sensation
all over again in one-light towns.
        Three days in Nebraska,
& a hundred calves come out bloody & new
        as Wahoo & Alma & Dunning hum

& glow, turned liked searchlights into
Colorado, where everyone's already wearing
        their lucky shoes.
It takes just one look at a boy from Ansley—
there is love & there is money
        & there is everything in between
        touched by both—
one look at the packs approaching the drag
in Imperial,
as first & second boy say hey & hey to third
& fourth—

Three days in Nebraska,
        & the bigger
the sentiment, the harder it falls, & all over
the dreams of the pretty
        end somewhere in New York City,
but just this one time,
                just these three days
in Nebraska, the boys are clicking their boots
& singing
        I wish I was here in Nebraska

                        —*Open Competition*

Zach Savich

On a Pose of Virgil's

Near its peak, the mountain requires nearly no
effort to climb. There is no sky behind the flags,
barges of pretty silt. Some wrestlers oil themselves
to prevent a grip, others rub grit on their skin

to help it. In the cartoon, Orpheus puts glasses on the back
of his head and walks in reverse. The pastor's white
collar is a foam neck brace. I am sorry to hear,
this morning, as I can't see the mug top through

the pouring steam, that there is nothing new in
philosophy: I meant to tell you a story but cannot
keep myself interested long enough to describe
the pinewoods exactly. I can never remember jokes,

but there were twenty-four flavors of syrup for
the soft-serve, as for an entire day of ice cream,
and a man near the summit holding his palms fast to
the grass, waiting for dew to come so he could wash.

—*Nominated by* The Iowa Review

Patrick Ryan Frank

Virginitiphobia

—The fear of rape

They took her out to the field in a new black truck
that smelled like apples and the denim

of a young man's thigh. They turned the engine off
but left the radio on, the headlights lighting

the woods to the west, toward the mountains, then
to California. They laid her down

and tied her hands over her head with field-grass.
She could have pulled them free, no problem,

ripped the roots right out of that soft dark dirt.
They told her she was beautiful.

They took off their shirts. She saw the black of their arms
backlit in gold by the truck's headlights.

One of them started to crack a joke, but stopped
halfway in. They took off her shoes

and touched her ankles, but only barely. She waited
for them to lift the hem of her skirt

but they were scared and it was cold out there.
She arched her back and held her breath,

eyes closed, but they kept saying they were sorry.
She told them to shut the fuck up, and if

they started to cry, she'd kill them and take the truck
and no one in town would ever know.

While they were kicking off their jeans, so slowly,
she listened to the radio

and the cicadas whirring like the circular saws
in the high-school shop, and a distant hum

that might have been a train if any trains
still ran anywhere nearby.

It must have been a plane somewhere way up
overhead, though she couldn't tell

because it was cloudy and dark, which bothered her;
she'd wanted them to see her face

moonlit and cold, staring up as they did it,
impossible to ever forget.

—*Nominated by* Boxcar Poetry Review

Rebecca Morgan Frank

Rescue

I.

Santo Tomas Internment camp, Manila

The hero arrives in an armada, years after you begin dreaming of him in black and white.

Armies stamp through your sleep, dole out chocolate, dried milk with a chalkiness
you long for.

In daylight hours you let your baby's face grow into a young man,
turn sounds of crying into words, and answer *chores, homework, grounded:*

You long to punish someone.

Men die for talking back. You collect retorts, place them in a bamboo box
that took days for you to make.

Some nights they come on horseback, charge and sweep you up, as if you were a girl, a
damsel, a princess. You wake, shamed, in sweat.

Other times they throw you a sword and you fight back. You pin the officer's sleeve
with the blade and make him stand until he falls in fatigue.

This is what it is to be weak.

You have seen strong men become bone, beggar, betrayer.

You dream of when you were a small boy, crying in a dorm in Hong Kong. No one comes. Then footsteps. Your dead mother vanquished by each strike of the cane.

Once you rescued a starved dog from a man with a stick.
On the walk home, it bit you, drawing blood.

God damn dog. Your waking words. The fleet has come. Or tomorrow, the fleet will come.
Every night, the fleet comes.

II.

What do I know about rescue?
The dead possum with her babies writhing in the bloody mess
a car made on impact?

How I got on the school bus and left them there, drowning in blood?

The time a girl pulled me out of the back of a pickup—
my belly full of pills—and drove me to the hospital?

The way it was never spoken of again?
Here is what rescue looks like in a photograph:
A sea of starved faces, a General:

MacArthur rescues my grandfather from internment.

I don't know what it is to be confined from life.
To be worthy of an army, of thousands of prayers back home.

What do I know about rescue?

Or the lack of it, as I was pinned to a bed.
Or later, chained to the near dead.

Who wants to hear these tales of local losses, of misplaced sacrifice?
Small parts of ourselves scalped, carried off by the victor.
The ones we had been trying to rescue.

What do I know about rescue, how to go in and do the job
and then leave?

MacArthur never moved into the camp and became a prisoner.
What is it about leaving I don't understand?

III.
  after Nelly Sachs

We the rescued carry forth your burdens. We take them
in flight across the South China Sea, the Philippine Sea, the islands between.

We beat the tin can of our enclosure, the failing wing,
the sing song of an engine dying. We drop ourselves into the white stretch

of our task, each grain a mask of who we have become. The sun
glares against our teapot of a temper, the whistling grows:

When will we be rescued? We the rescued report that you
have not returned us to ourselves. The plants are dying all around you.

Where is the water, the secret potion, the band-aid in the first aid,
the white apron, the history of helpers, the stethoscope, the doctor's

note: excuses for ourselves and everybody else. Resuscitated
blame. Why have you not come?

We the rescued are the ones already dead, the ones you said
had returned. We the rescued come postage paid. Bury us, take us

back to our soils. There is no place that does not call us home.
We are skinless, eyeless, we have no tongue. Can you hear us?

We the rescued rely on memory. You cannot forget
what follows you like a low dust, settling across

the tables and shelves, the back of the chair, whitening your hair.
We are everywhere you have not been. Do you feel us sticking

the elevator door? We the rescued, we are waiting. Can you
not hear our songs? How have you never come?

—*Nominated by* Guernica: A Magazine of Politics and Art

Brady Rhoades

Cesar Vallejo Is Dead

It's snowing in Santiago de Chuco and no one can
believe it, not the lonesome, backroad dogs or the insane.
The stars blew up, says a man
standing at the window in his socks. The world is changing;
those twins, hope and dread, snip each other's wounds
and show them off in vases. The vases are clay and the earth is breaking
off in pieces. Cesar Vallejo is dead, technically,
non-ambulatory, not there
in a winged-back chair in a book-filled room, but it's snowing
in Santiago de Chuco, and no one can believe it.

—*Nominated by* The Antioch Review

Diana Woodcock

Survivor

For Ngawang Sangdrol, Tibetan nun, released after eleven years

I walk beside the lake, late afternoon, waves restless and seagulls drowsy in sun along
its shore. Five cormorants on the decaying pier allowing me to watch them watching
for fish, shadows under shadows on the water. If I hold a sprig of rosemary to my nose
and inhale deeply, for a moment flesh will not burn. The chinaberry tree with its
wrinkled stone tells of its own hard journey: pride of India transplanted here; its
transformation imminent—fragrant purple petals on slender stalks. The otherwise
useless chaulmoogra yields an acrid oil that eases leprosy. Once, at the foot of a live
oak, I broke down and wept. Acorn cups were scattered throughout the woods,
turned up by the gods to catch rain for squirrels and quail to drink. All things find
their place. I come back to settle before the fire, drawn like the pandora sphinx moth
to the candle in the window. I slice the carambola into five equal pieces, five
cormorants on the pier, five women screaming, five beatings each day, and the cattle
prods. The Chinese prison guards went home at the end of their shifts to wives and
daughters. A phantom orchid in moist pinewoods feasts on forest duff—the fungus
in its roots a saving grace.

—Open Competition

Rhett Iseman Trull

Everything from That Point On

I.
All day the gulls dove, cries unsynchronized,
throats clinching every note as tightly as their bills

pincered quivering fish. The morning wind, spiked
with salt, stung our eyes as the sun slashed its light

across the numb horizon. *I guess this is mine now,* you said,
by default, drumming your chewed fingernails

with a hollow *ruc-a-tuc, ruc-a-tuc* on the bumper
of your father's truck, our reflection skewed in its dents.

And everything from that point on was slow motion:
the rest of the day spreading between us without words,

sunbathers coming and going, building their castles
until the tide slithered in to crush the towers in its grip.

Then the cooler air, clouds wisping thin, the last
of the fishermen reeling in, and the loon on one leg

letting the pink wings of sunset molest her feather by feather.

II.
Alone, under the cold fist of the moon and backed by hazy winks
of distant hotel lights, you slogged in calf-deep, the waves

gutting the ocean floor, sloshing its dregs against
you. From the shore I memorized

each splintered shell, each man-of-war, each muscle
you didn't flinch. Without ceremony, you slung the urn

out past the breakers, its lid tipping, dark tail of ashes
trailing. As you returned, the chill of the night

trembling through you, the smell of the brine in your hair,
I knew this would be the end for us. Your green eyes were pale,

scaled of their usual laughter. You swung from your loss,
gills straining. I loved you most in that moment, knowing

even as I slipped my arm up the back of your shirt, hooking us
together, that you were about to cut me loose to spare me

the tightening of the line, the bruise of sudden air.

—Open Competition

Melanie Carter

January

Already the starlings the wind whips
eastward are circling back
like a crown to their beginning.

On the ground below, the headstones
turn even the quiet maples
into chiseled monuments, sculpted boughs.

If one dark bird could grant
a wish, I'd ask to see the scepter
that directs this flight, that carves

a track so clearly in the air
these birds could fall into their sleep
and weave themselves back

to barren branches (their name alone
could make small sparks sing
in the fine trees, these tall trees).

I want to say that the man who could be king
is already my father (fine bones;
tall enough even to press his head

against the fragile hat these birds
are making with their thorny wings).
But he is gone, and the villagers have all gone

home and hung up their black coats.
I had not thought possible this plenty,
these songs unfastened from the empty trees.

—*Nominated by* The Gettysburg Review

Mary Kiolbasa

Hildegard of Bingen

1

New birds, just discovering their wings, the flock, they have wings coming out of their wings. The sun never touches them—the geese are old deceivers: We shoot them in the fall.

2

Their eggs come out oblong: I make perfect breaks and separate yolks with one hand. The white comes off clean, the yolk so bright it blinds us. I cook them hard in butter.

Balanced on one end, the thick end, when the moon is right: we did it on the porch in autumn. We froze the eggs first.

In the sheer white clear, that wheel of egg, the birds winged there and fell. We shot them down by ones. They flocked on the brink of floods. The feathers precipitated. The geese were flooding.

3

The North Wind pushed; the birds goosed. Eggs grew scarce. We ate liver to enhance our perception in the white times. Eating goose liver is nice. From its blood we learned to hear, our insides moving in our guts. We need livers and navels to hold it all back.

4

Lucifer was born with wings first and grew scales later. He shed feathers in the arctic and the scales grew in as fire, the fire cold. He laid eggs there; they froze.

He feels tired most often. He runs to pass the time: His knees hurt. He can't sleep. He is coming down with something. He is thick with amyloids. His blood vessels are gaseous. His sight is lacking like the dead. He can scarcely contain himself.

He eats the hearts out: the geese heart contains the whole body. The stomach claims the power of the creature, and when he chews the bones, the geese refill with marrow. They cannot walk, all thighs and knees, the wings baked hot, honey fresh—he is weak from the soft food.

5

The earth is surrounded by wings and jaws.

Inside the jaws, Lucifer is building a city for us to eat. Nothing exists there but rotisserie ovens. His city will be swept away when the darkness is ready. There is no way to measure this, as it is measureless.

It is cold and the corners are filled with dampness, odor, smoke. The fumes spread out. The geese flesh is putrid, peels off clean. We like the skin the best; it is delicious.

Lucifer made clothes for us from the skins, wove geese ribs into suits. He was mourning:

> *Eve in a sundress: jealous of her clothes, he looked down at his feather pocks. He tried to drown her, but she grew wings. He brought her to the building. He spit fountains upon her. She sprouted wings from her wings. She flew.*

6

The mighty city! He adorned it with mountains and Buddhas. He made a mirror. An outstretched wing flew through it. We saw ourselves perfect there, all navel and thigh. We sat in the silence of this.

7/8/9

Things we saw in the mirror:

    1. A piece of marble and a door to the city.

    2. A leopard with human eyes and bear claws.

    3. A hawk-handed man in a wooden suit.

    4. Three ladies in a swimming pool on top of the city, growing roots and singing.

    5. A man with lion feet. He has fish scales and three sets of wings, mirrors
         on his wings. A head protrudes from the stomach, looks down at his feet,
         ponders the lion. He flies with two wings. He is filled with delicious fruit.

10

On cosmic order:

> *"Just as eternity had no origin before the beginning of the world, it will have no*
> *end after the end of the world; the world's beginning and end will be enclosed,*
> *so to speak, in a unique cycle of understanding."*

This should be noted as significant: geese fly in circles before they are shot. They are restless and the world arises. But when the clouds have cleared from the mirror in the city of their bones, when we are stuffed to the brim on their livers and skins, when Lucifer is so full of the hearts he is ready to burst, the golden leopard head, as it appears on necklaces, will bear Lucifer's sign.

He gave it only once before:

A child possessed within the womb, the child born goosed, head first, chafes the canal with his beak, his long neck, but no wings and covered in scales. Born all thighs and knees and neck. The mark: and, like 3 legless geese in a row, it was never known before.

—Open Competition

Karen Rigby

The Lover

A film by Jean-Jacques Annaud, 1992
Excerpts from Marguerite Duras

The shuttered room a mind's throw
    from the truant girl flashing sequined heels

linen and lipstick   oxcarts
        fried bread
           the Chinese district
    her body as shorthand
    for what his body mistook for love—

you knew the lovers would fail but nothing stops
    the double-timed insouciance

        leaving mother and brothers
    a blindsight   the plantation

hammered to its slant foundation.

The victrola's fox-trot one more static to bear.

*

Because hunger traced the Mekong.
Because water broke
                    the salt-row harvest.

Because wind fluttered the girl's neckline

            Indochina minted on your tongue.

Marguerite Duras wrote *there are no seasons in that part of the world…
no spring, no renewal*

            no sound for the girl's hand releasing the rail,
the ferry an image you held in that humid air.

                                    *

Fortune.   Fever.

The lover twice her age In the colony
                    unthinkable

            this.

The alley patterned the wall in submarine blooms.

The girl returned
            root-bound
                    to the bachelor's room,

her body betraying its grammar,
the bone rose, the notched zero.

*

1929 Saigon
rehearsed the girl

for the canopy viewed
from the footbridge:

his wedding silk brocade.

*

Whiffs of burnt sugar drift into the room,
the smell of roasted peanuts,
Chinese soups, roast meat,

herbs, jasmine, dust, incense, charcoal fires,
they carry fire
about in baskets here,

it's sold in the street, the smell of the city
is the smell of the villages upcountry,
of the forest . . .

*

Marguerite was the French girl
writing the snaked road / scent swarming /
limbs slickened with resins / the lover raising
a palmful of water / after love
you enter and leave / you leave writing
it was already too late.

*

Out of lung sacs.
Out of blood. Mosquito nets.
Out of mornings in Sa Dec
      the glamour of the girl
           grew separate from the house
               flooded with voices

the river's clockwork   sunburned trees
the scissors inside her singing *the sea, the immensity*. . .

—*Open Competition*

Angela Vogel

Love Song for Manga

You're the girl I love, the girls I love,
Bishôjo conflated with *Moe*.
I wanna hold your *mangaka-*
drawn hand, go post-apocalyptic
for you. You're the worrisome line on my palm,
the box too small for no.10 mail.
You're a graveyard of catalogues
in manga cafés, the inkspot
where fandom blow moula & *kissa*.
At times you are webmanga,
worldmanga, AmericanGirl manga.
Your *chibi* are alien, techno,
they hold the Lord's roof.
They are *ecchi* and modded,
they are nature's hosanna.
I'm your best shot at reaching
the sky above *yonkoma*,
your ticket bye-bye to *shôjo-ai*,
my moonpie. So what
if we fight? The physics are toon.
Those that need to hang

from cliffs do. Oh sweatdrop
pursed with oodles of yen,
how many flaps with wild Western men
pitching tents? And what then?

—Open Competition

Ethan Stebbins

Porn

Porn was a dark place,
buried at the back of my father's closet.
You went alone, parting the folds
of brown and navy blazers, past
shoes and luggage and ancient dumbbells,
the silk tongues of a rotary tie-wheel.
Inside one box inside another

in the dark. And it was real,
the way it entered the working mouth
of the VCR, the little whine
the film wheels made. It was always
the same: a clean, well-lit room,
double bed, bedside table
and table lamp. The door opened.

But first the empty room.
I remember exactly: a velvet, airbrushed
mountianscape hung above the bed.
Solitude and bare extremities.
It was winter, a little cabin glowed

in the distance. You knew from the smoke
it must be warm in there.

—Nominated by New York University

Weston Cutter

You Could Call It a Shift

It's a beach: after   the dreams of heat
        in a too hot room   in a country
I came to because: because: it was there
        though *because* is never enough
            nor is   the yellowgray of
            sunrise following   the orangepink
of sunset: or the man,   beach's edge,
        untethered moon up and   left, straight
ahead   enough stars   still   to believe in
        something: the man: large arms:
manufacturing nets   from splintery remains,
from   broken bowlines,   windwrecked
        wooden ribs: not even nets: but:
like the man   ____once loved   who made the painting
of the heart   on the painting   of the fire
            on the painting   of the fingers
            on the painting   of the stone
            on the painting

                of some stranger's
                        face:

none of it is enough: not   the discernable sigh
from some   still-sleeping form,   away   from
     the waves' tilt: not the man   making nets from old
breakings: and how moving   closer   there's a hole the size
of a thought, a fist, a face: the face you meant to make
               when he showed you the painting
      and said *see? I never meant any of it*:   how *enough* is not even enough:
and how   when you ask the man   now   about
       the net, how there's   too big   a hole   in it
to gather much   he doesn't   from his work look
       up: says *this catches all I need*:   how
     each wave takes whatever   the last left:

—Nominated by Virginia Tech

Anne Marie Rooney

Sabbath for a Dry Season

It was not raining, had only
once rained, would never rain
again. Across the river, the sun
made angels appear stoic.

      In a dark wet room two people
      burn holes in each other. In Styx.
      In the middle of a dope dream
      and the walls are very quiet
      and the sky is burning

      and Out There
      in the thin night
      a girl unhooks her bones

*

If Love is

    strings and bark
    the backs of bows hitting rock
    ankles caught at the bottom of a bed
    Jupiter and his 63 moons

    If faith is

Dumb Luck.
Sticky lotteries in a pick-up truck.

          *

They write books about this sort of magic: It is dark
forever and then it is light. Deer legs buckle into
two shooting stars.

    No one is bleeding behind that tree.
    No one is writing poems to stop

    that make-believe blood.

        —Open Competition

Will Smiley

I Went

I went with the man to his building.
When we walked in, I saw a pool table.

The man's partner was serving me the meal I had been
promised, and there was a waitress behind the bar
putting glasses away. One of them dropped in front of me
and shattered.
                    It was hard to make out
what the man's partner was saying, but I
was eating. This would be a wonderful room, I thought,
for fucking, and had a vision of a couple
copulating right there before my eyes.

Help me, the waitress said.
I peered over the bar and found her
with the dust and the shards
arrayed at her feet.

Help us, the man's partner said.
I tried to remember what the culprit looked like,
I tried to replay the offending scene in my mind, I saw the dust

blowing across the parking lot into the wheat field adjacent,
I saw a man standing at the fringe of the field vanish
without turning to acknowledge us.

Am I going to die, I asked.
I live in this neighborhood, the man's partner said,
and I don't think you will. Then she told me
she had just taken her daughter
to the Windmill, and it was perfectly safe.
Have you ever been there? I told her I hadn't,
and she led me up the stairs.

—Open Competition

Lisa McCullough

The Boar Roast

Duncan, Kentucky

Not what you'd call a going concern.
Backed against a low ridge, a mile or so
east of the river separating Mercer from
Washington County, the town—

by the gazetteer just a "populated place,"
no tree-lined streets of homes, no
businesses, the ground unfit for cash
crops, horses or tobacco—

has nothing you'd want to stop for.
A few beat-up sooty houses too close
to the two-lane highway, skewed porches,
scabbed yellow paint, the front yards

piled with what doesn't work anymore.
Behind them, a shack once used to quarter
slaves for auction, gaunt rafters,
power lines. Then the ridge, one side

half-recovered from clearcutting.
The gas station has a broken window,
the man at the pump's broken too,
it's an effort to look him in the eye

when you ask directions. If you'd taken
U.S. 25 through the Cumberland Gap,
you'd have come upon the Bluegrass
the way Boone and his men did,

all of sudden there below you, country
you might think, as they must have,
no one could be poor in. Families
trying their luck, homesteads, roads

to the settlements, commerce
on the river, the corn in tassel
for the mill, rails laid to the coal,
the mines dug and died in.

That February the brothers had quit work
on the cabin they were building on the ridge,
took the truck and headed south.
From where the dime store used to be,

you'd have seen them driving down
out of the jack pines, heard the tires
roll off the crusher run, go quiet on the
blacktop, ice in the ditch, in the turns

no sun, for many miles the limestone
karsts on both sides like enormous
marrow bones exposed in the road cuts.
I-75 through Tennessee and Georgia, then

Route 27 to the Everglades. A gradual
coming out from under—there are
more stations on the radio, the talk
about the cabin warms, they remember

how they'd witched for water,
dug the well and capped it, sited the
foundation, laid the footers, the work
backbreaking but coming along. The logs,

salvage from around the state, are
hundreds of years old and all hand-
hewn by men like them. The house
Mary Todd's half-brothers left

to join the rebels, Charles Floyd's place
in the Pennyrile. In the Purchase a Scot,
shouting from the door to hush the dogs,
sees the Cherokee under a pall of dust

walking out of the Carolinas. The wood
chained and lifted up, loaded on a flatbed,
hauled to a friend's shed and stacked. Imagine,
after all that, how good it felt to be in a

swamp buggy in the dazzle, holding guns
instead of shovels, not thinking of the 12-degree
grade of the road to the cabin that'll be
hell to get up when it snows, with nothing

to do for a while but drink beer and hunt boar.
Their happiness and the black thing
hanging head-down from a poplar tree
for bleeding and the photographs,

then dressed, freezer-wrapped, and iced
for the drive home. Ahead a thousand miles is
cloud cover, the dirt floor, the ridge shadow
sliding over the windshield. In May, the cabin

pretty much done, they soaked the carcass
three days in cider, dug the pit and lined it
with river rock for the roasting. Everyone
made welcome at the table the friends

of friends from out of town, everyone
brought what they had to celebrate
the end of work and the view from up there,
the valley and the farther hills,

where you could see the green haze coming
as spring took hold. There were stories
about the killing, the Derby on TV, two
unweaned kittens in a paint bucket

for the children to play with.
At sundown, the brothers threw gas
on the bonfire and lit it,
and a heavy man in shorts, his legs

clutched with varicose veins,
pulled a chair near and opened
his fiddle case. Others came with their
guitars and a banjo, soft under

the voices you could hear them
tune the strings, and the darkness over them
and over all they do, that won't give way,
gives way now, a little, to the music.

—*Nominated by the University of Maryland*

Chloë Honum

Directing the Happy Times

Think April, late, when all things tilt, quiver
with color and rain. Begin hibiscus, drip

like a woman in wet clothes. With deeper curve
magnolia, you ache and brown. Last drop

knock down the honeybee; on three, it bobs,
a cork in water, that's its time to shine.

Wisteria, study the air where it throbs.
Be amethyst. Focus. I'll need the vine

to fully engage the tree, lilies to white
one by one as mother walks the lane.

It must be this precise, or simply put
she'll get distracted, fail to read her line.

She will not laugh, the waiting stagehands' cue:
(lights down) Enter the shadows who carry you.

—*Open Competition*

Jenny Johnson

Ladies' Arm Wrestling Match at the Blue Moon Diner

On a red booth with Rose, right hand bracing a beer,
left elbow dismantling a pastoral, we shout into the throng—

In a leather body suit, Stiletto squeezes, insists, reconciles,
hazel eyes working overtime on the fist of her opponent.

Under the table there's a penalty, "Left foot off the ground!"
A python en-circling her bicep, Sidewinder hisses like this: Sss Sss Sss

Then, Cheryl, golden as Carhartts, softening us,
"My grandma always told me if life gives you lemons

throw 'em away." And so, we loosen. We shuffle off sore tendons.
Tuesdays. And insults cat-called out Chevy windows.

Clinking whiskey glasses, we wipe away sweat and
old flames who only leave muscles warm in daydreams.

Before the heat begins again, I have this vision
of a kid kicking up dust for hours in the road.

All I ever found in the gravel was the paper body,
what the gartersnake shed. Take off that old suit, tonight.

Even as your good arm shudders to the mat
like the waning crescent meeting the mouth of the Shenandoah.

In new skin, come back again and again. Own this acreage.
This new ground rippling under rolled sleeves.

—Open Competition

Brian Christian

The Present

It's good practice. It keeps the flies off,
the phoenixes down. It keeps the butter
soft, the cocksure cock hard. It's a
strengthening agent, toughens you up. It makes
you brittle and/or suffer. It makes you a
man but not in that way. It forces you
to accept a number of contradictory propositions.
Its logic unfolds from invisible axioms.
It produces color, but only as a secondary
quality grounded in texture. It takes up
space but only as a secondary quality grounded
in color. It folds, unfolds, sags. It
hates you. That's what it does. It folds
you up like a blintz, an origami balloon,
a fortune teller. It plays wastrel to you,
minstrel to you. It puts a head on your
shoulders, knocks it off. It puts hair on your
back, waxes it. It takes your fingerprint
and runs off with it. It takes forever
to get anything done around here. It
takes a lot out of you. It gives you a
headache, a heartache, a hernia. It takes
a village to raise your child, a gurney to

raise your body, courage to raise your
voice. It's a membrane between all
that there is and nothing. It cost me
a fortune so I hope you like it.

—Nominated by the University of Washington

Michael Davis

Boethius in New Jersey

I've never found it easy picturing
Boethius in a stone cell, walls bare
and unsympathetic, as he drives out
the Muses. He's more the middle-aged man
with a receding hairline somewhere
east of Philadelphia, his eyes open
for a sign to any bridge—the Ben Franklin,
the Walt Whitmam—any way out.
Each long avenue looks the same,
bowling alleys and strip clubs,
gaudy bars with their ladies nights,
discount mattress stores, breakfast joints.
This morning at Wegman's supermarket
a flock of geese circled and circled,
but the yellow-lined parking spaces
never receded, never evaporated to reveal
the wetland the birds were hard-wired
to seek out, so they settled, probably,
on a small patch of grass, some cattails
pushing up through brown winter, in the middle
of that new business park down the road

from the Holiday Inn. Boethius drifts
through an intersection called "Circle"
for the sixth time tonight, each road
that strikes out from the tangle
of traffic signals has five lanes, a road
that stretches all the way to Atlantic City
or somewhere worse, where teenagers
roll back and forth between 7-Eleven franchises
and rock anthems, between dark
parentless houses in all these neighboring
lookalike towns. Oh Muse of asphalt,
oh Muse of strikes and gutters, Muse
of menthol cigarettes, Muse of high school girls
trying to pass as five years older,
Muse of thirtysomething women
trying to pass as ten years younger,
Muse of souped up Pontiacs, Muse
of hopeful part-time models, Muse in
a low-cut Eagles jersey, Muse of sports bars,
Muse of shopping malls, Muse stuck
in traffic at rush hour, glancing sideways
at me across the steering wheel and biting
your lower lip, flirting out of boredom,
Muse of the long commute, of donut shops,
of 32-ounce big gulp sodas, how did you
end up here? Why don't you just leave?

You're no use to me,

my brother has cancer, my sister
is on the phone in tears, she's crying
in the coat room, I'm next to her,
I'm miles away, every billboard promises
credit solutions or acres of auto malls.
The Muses here are just pretty girls serving me
cold beer in front of flatscreen TVs.

They want to leave, too, but can't think
of anywhere to go. Boethius, come clean,
I think you made the whole story up,
the grief, the exile, the prison,
then you wrote yourself back out. I don't want
Lady Philosophy, I don't want Reason,
the signs here are no good, I've been driving for hours,
what I need now is some kind of map,
or a big-eyed girl in skin-tight jeans
—put on some extra mascara, please,
and eyeliner, pout a little with your lips—
to give me directions or simply
stay awake and talk to me, say out loud
all the reasons she'll never leave me.

—Open Competition

Malachi Black

Traveling by Train

And faster past another frozen river,
the brambles, shrubs, and underbrush of dead
woods and the garbage that was left behind
by runaways and skunks: the plastic bags
and twine, shoes beside forgotten brands
of beer whose cans, so battered by the weather,
have all but disappeared—like the whiteness
of a smoke after it's cleared. And you've been on
this train too long to know the time: you're lost
between the meter and the desperate rhyme
of clacking tracks. Home is nothing here.
You're gone and in the going; can't come back.

—Open Competition

Martha Greenwald

Other Prohibited Items

> *"try not to over-think these guidelines."*
> —Southwest.com Carry-on Tips

No to his bassoon. No to their cricket bat.
No to your robot, her corkscrew, that hatchet.
Good traveler, whose children might be overjoyed—

Next trip, please procure toys that resemble toys.
Policy does not ban pink princess/pirate swords
But for security, we confiscate all backstories

(Though adaptations are few). Item: one wrench
From a beloved uncle's workbench, pilfered
After his funeral, just before the flight. Lost thanks

For his kindnesses, the raucous Christmas pranks—
Although he taught his nephew the lathe, relinquish
The memento at our checkpoint. Item: rose oil,

Decanted by monks, four ounces in a faceted flacon.
Rare, the passenger whispers, hushed, as if pleading
To the lover for whom the secret gift was intended—

Well, her kiss may *be* sublime but no to the perfume's
Ounce of excess; and no to the antique drawknife
Despite its moonstone handle, studded with marcasite.

Again, mid-shift, a woman about to board a red-eye
Puts her Ziploc on the x-ray conveyor, then flusters
When we screen the bag's contents. The bottles warm

Our gloved hands. Milk rivulets dampen our sleeves.
However, her infant waits at the destination, so toss
Her bottles to the take-bin, foremilk already separating

From hindmilk. No to her umbrella, unruly, floral.
Sorry—storm phobias never justify hollow finials.
No exceptions for the sentimental or exceptional.

Our take-bins swell with keepsakes decades misplaced,
With longings for the heft of a snowglobe balanced
On a small palm. Look inside—old Snow White

Sleeps in a dubious solution. No to her domed sky's
Blizzard. No to the castle, no to apples. Witches lurk
In these woods, and every poisoned pie is gooseberry.

—*Open Competition*

Abraham Burickson

At the Barbecue Joint, Taylor, Texas

Across the bar the woman has fixed her eyes on me.
Gnarled old woman, and I shiver a little

because she's not moving, and the only time
I've ever been that still a cold hand
dragged its way up my spine. Dry stare. Same eyes

as my grandmother when she sat in the sun,
nothing to say, flakes of skin dropping to her lap

like sawdust. *I miss you already*, she'd say as soon
as I arrived. But that was all. And the old cowboy's
telling me they stuff the sausage here, in the back,

which is a making-the-best-of-things. I did that once
in the hills south of Quito, the fat matron pushing

my hands into a bucket of blood, weeping, stuffing
meat into an intestine: *My sons have left me, me olvidaron,*
I am alone here in this valley, this valley of women

awaiting letters and money that never come. And now
the sausage comes, cold and tough, and the woman

still staring, slowly crushing a beer can, and the cowboy's
finished with the jukebox, but no music comes. Even
the brisket is dry, and, though I am still hungry,

I pay my bill and drive to the gas station, where
the spreading reds and oranges make all those big cars

shine. Which is what my grandmother was doing,
I suppose, shining. Or waiting to. And that's something
when there's nothing left to say. Just sit in the car

and watch snow geese cut holes in the light, a perforation
for night, and I think *where they're going I will go*. I float

the car back to the road but I forgot the pump
still in the tank, and it goes with the slightest *snap*,
and the sound of water hitting the ground. But it's not

water, just the attendant waving his arms, then shrinking,
darkening, as I pull onto the highway, into the wind,

into the flicking on of headlights, and the geese all gone,
or it's too dark to see them, and I forgot which way they
were going. And migration never was my business anyway.

*—Nominated by the University of Texas
Michener Center for Writers*

Josephine Yu

The Thing You Might Not Understand

when I tell you the man whose children I babysat in college
cornered me on the deck after the party and copped a feel

is how his eyes looked drunk, glassy and sad,
and how his smile tilted apologetically but his body

was straight and formal, as if we were dignitaries shaking hands,
or how he held my breast as gently as I cupped his daughter's head

the first time I washed her in the kitchen sink,
rubbing the cradle cap from her hair with baby oil,

palming warm water over her head, pale silk strands
swirling like fine crackling in the glaze of old porcelain,

the veins of her eyelids a faint calligraphy on vellum,
the extant manuscript that would reveal, if we could translate it,

a treatise on forgiveness, or canticles of grace,
a tune we sometimes hum, unaware, under our breath

as we walk to the mailbox, or fill a birdfeeder with seed,
or lower a man's hand and lead him back into his house.

—Nominated by Florida State University

Jonathan Rice

Momento Mori

Your daughter showed me the ones you kept
as proof that you sold those parents the pictures

they asked for, their instructions in brackets
at the glossy-white margins:

[*Blush/Powder*] an infant whose eyes could not be shut.
Another, a girl who would be ten this year, [*Dress/Blanket*]

glowed in her yellow gown, over-exposed
after the run red light and sutured mother. [*None*] worse

than the rest: gone in utero, its flesh still womb-water taut,
the wrested expression of its purpled face not to be believed.

Never an explanation. She said the parents were led
out a side door, released to the mornings or late afternoons

of their loss, to take themselves home before you arrived.
No one stayed for that. And the body, if what remained

could be called a body, was left alone in the darkened room
of failed birth, and that often, you had to wash it yourself:

lower it gently to the stainless sink, cupping the neck,
careful of the soft skull, the water warmed to your wrist.

*

Only now do I understand why you let us wander
alone so many nights through the warm fields and stables,

and know what you hoped for from the tallgrass pastures
while her father slept, drunk and barely rising

from the couch. I return to these thoughts when I wake
and stare with fear and then wonder at my wife's stomach.

In the morning dark I am waiting with a hand at her navel,
for the subtle kick, a heel swung out from the suspended dream.

There is nothing to do but wait. In the doctor's office,
we watch the shape of our child form in the black and white

resin of sound on the little monitor we all must look up to see.
The sonographer's face is as impassive as a mechanic's.

Then flow chart and pen scratch, the transducer lifted,
and our daughter recedes, kilohertz at a time.

*

Those first years after your daughter, I knew a girl
whose boyfriend was in the Army, then gone for war.

He came home twice before mortars or the broil
of a blown up vehicle kept him. The last time he left

she was sleeping. This was their agreement, since
she could not willingly let him go. Rumor was she quit

the pill weeks before his last furlough, then met him
at the airport and took him home. And of course,

of course she didn't tell. You'd have to know her
as I knew her then, to see how years piled under her eyes.

Her hair thinned with waiting. The boy was healthy
when he came, and she brought him around.

The other story followed. She could not leave him
in his crib to sleep, but woke to check his breathing

every hour, obsessed to know that he lived, even when
he wailed to be changed, or took to her breast, or began

to crawl a little. When she turned away, he was gone.
He'd been on the bed. He had been lying on the bed

near her. With her hand on his back, she'd counted
breath-falls and minutes of heartbeat. When he woke,

she would tell him another story of his father
coming home. He was gone. She'd left to take a call

and come back and found him face down in the folds
of a plastic bag between the bed and wall.

When I'm driving home after work, and think of this,
I swerve to keep course, and sometimes wander

the aisles of superstores filled with gadgets and toys,
plush clothes pressed to the shape of six months,

nine weeks, one year, stand gawking at self-rocking cribs,
the crystalline rows of bottles and modestly packaged

breast pumps, pacifiers and bibs with lion or chicken or frog
or innumerable constellations of stars stitched in their corners.

*

After your daughter showed me the snapshots
of what had been lost, neither of us asked why

anyone would want such a portrait. To frame
and have blessed, or keep locked and untouchable,

preserved like a promise held in the silences
of unspeakable memory, it didn't matter

to us then. We walked out together, toward
the stream at the edge of your land. It was

summer. The heat was unbelievable, even in
the coolest place we knew. We pulled off our shirts

and spread them under us to lie down.
Though there was no moon, we did not kiss

or touch each other, wanting only our own silence
in the scald of such knowledge we should not have.

—Open Competition

Acknowledgments

Seth Abramson's "Nebraska" previously published by *Poetry*

Michael Bazzett's "Clouds and Mountains" previously published by *Weber: The Contemporary West*

Malachi Black's "Traveling by Train" previously published by *AGNI Online*

Melanie Carter's "January" previously published by *The Gettysburg Review*

Adam Day's "Hiding Again, in London" previously published by *The Antioch Review*

Keith Ekiss's "Pima Road Notebook (II)" previously published by *Blackbird*

Clint Frakes's "Mystery Not Always Unkind" previously published by *Tinfish*

Patrick Ryan Frank's "Virginitiphobia" previously published by *Boxcar Poetry Review*

Rebecca Morgan Frank's "Rescue" previously published by *Guernica: A Magazine of Politics and Art*

Landon Godfrey's "Second-Skin Rhinestone-Spangled Nude Soufflé Chiffon Gown" previously published by *The Southeast Review*

Chloë Honum's "Directing the Happy Times" forthcoming in *Nimrod International Journal*

Eva Hooker's "Before the Spring in which the Forsythia Bloom and She Unravels All Her Charms, Mother Writes" previously published by *Harvard Review*

Anna Journey's "Adorable Siren, Do You Love the Damned?" previously published by *The Kenyon Review*

A portion of Aby Kaupang's "It Takes a Pillage to Sing a Strom Song" previously published by *The Laurel Review*

Steve Kistulentz's "The David Lee Roth Fuck Poem with Language Taken from *Van Halen I, 1984*, and The First Letter of the Apostle Paul to the Church at Corinth" previously published by *No Tell Motel*

Jennifer Militello's "Personality State: Prophet" previously published by *The Kenyon Review*

Darren Morris's "Counting Down the Night" previously published by *Memorious: A Journal of New Verse and Fiction*

Brady Rhoades's "Cesar Vallejo is Dead" previously published by *The Antioch Review*

Jonathan Rice's "Momento Mori" previously published by *Harpur Palate*

Karen Rigby's "The Lover" previously published by *Linebreak*

Anne Marie Rooney's "Sabbath for a Dry Season," previously published by *Parthenon West Review*

Zach Savich's "On a Pose of Virgil's" previously published by *The Iowa Review*

Will Smiley's "I Went" previously published by *NEO* (Portugal)

Alexandra Teague's "Adjectives of Order" previously published by *Slate*

Rhett Iseman Trull's "Everything from That Point On" previously published by *storySouth*

Diana Woodcock's "Survivor" previously published by *Nimrod International Journal*

Contributors' Notes

SETH ABRAMSON is the author of *The Suburban Ecstasies* (Ghost Road Press, forthcoming 2009), and a contributing author to *The Creative Writing MFA Handbook* (Continuum Publishing, 2008). Recent poems have appeared in *Poetry, Poetry Daily, jubilat,* and *LIT,* and are forthcoming in *New American Writing, Salmagundi, New York Quarterly, Pleiades, Subtropics,* and elsewhere. A graduate of Harvard Law School and a former public defender, Seth currently attends the Iowa Writers' Workshop.

MICHAEL BAZZETT is a poet and printmaker dividing his time between Minneapolis and San Miguel de Allende, Mexico, where he currently lives with his wife and two children. His work has appeared in *Green Mountains Review, The Chattahoochee Review, The MacGuffin, 32 Poems, Rattle, Weber: The Contemporary West,* and elsewhere.

MALACHI BLACK is literary editor of *The New York Quarterly* and a James A. Michener Fellow at the University of Texas at Austin's Michener Center for Writers. His work has recently appeared or is forthcoming in *AGNI Online, Indiana Review, The Iowa Review, Pleiades,* and elsewhere.

DREW BLANCHARD is a doctoral candidate in Irish Studies and twentieth century American literature at the University of Wisconsin-Milwaukee. His writing has appeared or is forthcoming in *Blue Canary, Notre Dame Review, An Sionach, Cream City Review,* and elsewhere.

ABRAHAM BURICKSON is a poet, architect, and conceptual artist. His poetry can be found in *Blackbird, Sycamore Review, New Orleans Review, Painted Bride Quarterly, Time Out Chicago,* and elsewhere. In 2001 he founded the experimental performance group Odyssey Works, a cross-genre collaborative that created day-long performances for extremely small audiences. He has received fellowships from the Millay Colony for the Arts and the Michener Center for Writers, where he recently received his M.F.A.

MELANIE CARTER's poems have been published in *The Antioch Review, The Spoon River Poetry Review, Shenandoah,* and other journals. She currently teaches writing at The American University in Cairo.

BRIAN CHRISTIAN's writing appears in literary journals such as *AGNI, Seneca Review,* and *Ninth Letter,* on the web at *Conjunctions* and *McSweeney's,* and in scientific journals such as *Cognitive Science.* Born in Wilmington, Delaware, Christian holds degrees in philosophy, computer science, and poetry from Brown University and the University of Washington, where he teaches.

WESTON CUTTER is from Minnesota and has had work recently in *Ninth Letter* and *The Duck and Herring Co.*

MICHAEL DAVIS lives with his wife and their two cats in Portland, Oregon. He works in the development office at Reed College.

ADAM DAY's work has appeared or is forthcoming in the T*he Kenyon Review, American Poetry Review, Antioch Review, Salmagundi,* and elsewhere. He helps coordinate the Sarabande Reading Series, and the Baltic Writing Residency in Latvia. He recently received a grant from the Kentucky Arts Council, and won the 2008 *Madison Review's* Phyllis Smart Young poetry prize and the 2008 St. Louis Poetry Center prize.

KEITH EKISS is the Jones Lecturer in Poetry at Stanford University for 2007–2009, and the past recipient of scholarships and residencies from the Bread Loaf and Squaw

Valley Writers' Conferences, Santa Fe Art Institute, Millay Colony for the Arts, and the Petrified Forest National Park. His poems and his translations of the Costa Rican poet Eunice Odio have appeared in *Blackbird, Gulf Coast, Mid-American Review, Modern Poetry in Translation, New England Review,* and elsewhere. He is the Acting Artistic Director for the Center for the Art of Translation in San Francisco.

CLINT FRAKES is a graduate of the Jack Kerouac School of Disembodied Poetics at the Naropa Institute and the Northern Arizona University Writing Program. He received his Ph.D. in creative writing from the University of Hawai'i in 2006. His recent work has appeared in *Bamboo Ridge, Hawai'i Pacific Review, Tinfish,* and *Language and Culture.* He received the James Vaughan and Peggy Ferris Awards for Poetry in 2006. He is the former chief editor of *Hawai'i Review* and *Big Rain.*

REBECCA MORGAN FRANK received her M.F.A. from Emerson College and is an Elliston Poetry Fellow at the University of Cincinnati. Her poetry has appeared or is forthcoming in *The Georgia Review, Ploughshares, Prairie Schooner,* and elsewhere. She has received a Tennessee Williams scholarship from the Sewanee Writers' Conference and a Nadya Aisenberg fellowship from the Writers' Room of Boston. She is a founding editor of the online journal *Memorious: A Journal of New Verse and Fiction.*

PATRICK RYAN FRANK has published poems in several journals including *Poetry, The North American Review, Rhino,* and *Carolina Quarterly.* He is the recipient of an Artist's Grant from the Massachusetts Cultural Council and two fellowships from the Fine Arts Work Center in Provincetown, Massachusetts. He studied theatre and poetry at Northwestern University and received his M.A. in poetry from Boston University. He lives in Austin, Texas, where he is pursuing an M.F.A. at the Michener Center for Writers at the University of Texas.

KERRI FRENCH has studied at UNC-Chapel Hill, UNC-Greensboro, and Boston University. Her poems have been featured on Sirius Satellite Radio and have been published in *Agenda, Brooklyn Review, Fugue, Natural Bridge,* and *Lumina.* She teaches in the Writing Program at Boston University and in the English Department at Mount Ida College.

LANDON GODFREY was born and raised in Washington, D.C., and now lives in Black Mountain, North Carolina, with her husband, Gary Hawkins. She works as a free-lance writer and artist. Her poems have appeared in various journals including *The Southeast Review, Lyric, Chelsea, The Beloit Poetry Review, The Cimarron Review,* and *POOL.*

MARTHA GREENWALD's poems have appeared in various journals including *Slate, The Threepenny Review, Poetry, Shenandoah, Dogwood,* and *The New England Review.* She is a former Wallace Stegner Fellow in Creative Writing and has received fellowships from both the North Carolina and Kentucky Arts Councils.

CHLOË HONUM grew up in New Zealand. She is an M.F.A. candidate at the University of Arkansas, where she directs the Writers in the Schools program. Her work is forthcoming in *Nimrod, Shenandoah, Crab Orchard Review,* and *The Paris Review.*

EVA HOOKER is Professor of English and Writer in Residence at Saint Mary's College, Notre Dame, Indiana. *The Winter Keeper,* a hand-bound chapbook (Chapiteau Press, Montpelier, Vermont, 2000), was a finalist for the Minnesota Book Award in poetry in 2001. Her poems have recently appeared in *The Harvard Review, Water-Stone, Orion, Agni Online, Web Conjunctions,* and *The Notre Dame Review.*

LUKE JOHNSON is a teaching fellow in the M.F.A. program at Hollins University. His poems have appeared or are forthcoming in *New York Quarterly, Georgetown Review, storySouth, Poet Lore,* and elsewhere. He lives in Roanoke, Virginia with a thirteen-year-old sheepdog that growls at sweet old ladies.

JENNY JOHNSON is an M.F.A. candidate at Warren Wilson College. She currently lives in Charlottesville, Virginia, where she is assistant director of The Young Writers Workshop of The University of Virginia.

ANNA JOURNEY is the author of *If Birds Gather Your Hair for Nesting* (University of Georgia Press, 2009), winner of the National Poetry Series. She is a Ph.D. candidate in creative writing and literature at the University of Houston, where she also serves as a poetry editor for *Gulf Coast.*

ABY KAUPANG is a graduate of Colorado State University. Her poetry has appeared or is forthcoming in *Verse, Denver Quarterly, Dusie, Parcel, The Laurel Review, Parthenon West, Aufgabe, 14 Hills, Interim, Caketrain,* and *Shampoo.*

MARY KIOLBASA is a graduate of Knox College and is currently pursuing an M.F.A. in Writing at the School of the Art Institute of Chicago.

STEVE KISTULENTZ is a doctoral candidate at the Florida State University, where he has twice been awarded the John Mackay Shaw Academy of American Poets Prize. His poems have appeared in numerous journals including *The Antioch Review, Black Warrior Review, Crab Orchard Review, New England Review, Caesura, New Letters, Quarterly West,* and others. He holds an M.F.A. from the Iowa Writers' Workshop, where he was the Joseph and Ursil Callan Scholar.

TRACEY KNAPP lives in San Francisco, where she works as a graphic designer. Most recently, her poems have appeared in *The Minnesota Review, No Tell Motel,* and *The Carolina Quarterly* Emerging Voices Issue. She holds an M.A. in English from Ohio University and an M.A. in poetry from Boston University.

PAUL LONGO lives in Portland, Oregon. A recovering engineer with a recent M.F.A. from the University of Arizona, he manages healthcare projects at a design firm.

CHRISTOPHER LOUVET's poems have appeared in *The Bitter Oleander, Tigertail: A South Florida Poetry Annual,* and online at *McSweeney's Internet Tendency.* He currently lives in Miami Beach.

CYNTHIA LOWEN is a graduate of Sarah Lawrence College's M.F.A. in Creative Writing Program and has served as an editor at Four Way Books. She has received a fellowship to the Fine Arts Work Center in Provincetown, Massachusetts, the "Discovery"/*Boston Review* Prize, the *Tin House*/Summer Literary Seminars Kenya Prize, and the *Inkwell* 11th Annual Poetry Prize. Her work has appeared or is forthcoming in *Barrow Street, Black Warrior Review, Boston Review, Inkwell, The Laurel Review, Lumina, Provincetown Arts,* and *Tin House,* among others. She lives in New York City.

ANGIE MAZAKIS received an M.A. from Ohio University. She was runner-up for the *New Letters Poetry Prize* in 2004 and received third prize for the Erskine J. Poetry Prize from *Smartish Pace* in 2006.

LISA MCCULLOUGH is a graduate of the University of Maryland's Creative Writing Program. Her poems have appeared most recently in *TriQuarterly* and *Tikkun.*

JENNIFER MILITELLO is the author of *History of the Always Pain,* winner of the 2007 Tupelo Press First Book Prize and forthcoming in 2009, and of the chapbook *Anchor Chain, Open Sail* (Finishing Line Press, 2006). Her poems have appeared in *Boston Review, The Kenyon Review, The New Republic, The North American Review, The Paris Review,* and *The Virginia Quarterly Review.* She has received fellowships from The New Hampshire State Council on the Arts, The Barbara Deming Memorial Fund, Writers at Work, and the Millay Colony for the Arts.

DARREN MORRIS is a graduate of the M.F.A. program at Virginia Commonwealth University. His poems have appeared in *The American Poetry Review, River Styx, Rattle,* and others. His fiction has been awarded a fellowship from The Virginia Commission for the Arts, and his collection of short stories is currently under consideration.

LISA OTTIGER was born in the Philippines and has lived in Hawai'i for the past twelve years. She recently completed her doctorate in English at the University of Hawai'i at

Manoa. "Rainlight" is from her dissertation, a novel in poetry titled *Sandugo: Blood Compact*. Other poems from the collection are forthcoming in Hawai'i Review.

HEIDI JOHANNESEN POON has received fellowships from Brown, the Iowa Writers' Workshop and the MacDowell Colony. Her work has appeared more recently in *Black Warrior Review, Nimrod,* and *The McSweeney's Book of Poets Picking Poets*.

MARCIA POPP is a retired university professor and the author of several textbooks and biographies. Her poem "strike up the band" will be included in a narrative collection to be published by Black Zinnias Press in the fall of 2008. "comfort in small rooms" from this collection won the 2008 Robert G. Cohn prose poetry award. Her poetry has also appeared in *Avocet: A Journal of Nature Poems*.

BRADY RHOADES's poems have appeared in *The Antioch Review, Baltimore Review, Faultline, Louisville Review, Windsor Review,* and the anthologies *Bear Flag Republic: Prose Poems and Poetics from California* and *Homage to Vallejo*. He recently completed a themed book of poems, many of which have been published, titled *Insomnia (notes from expeditions)*. He lives in Fullerton, California.

JONATHAN RICE's poems appear or are forthcoming in *Colorado Review, Crab Orchard Review, New Delta Review, Sycamore Review, AGNI* Online, *Georgetown Review, pacificREVIEW, Notre Dame Review,* and *Witness*. He was selected for the 2008 *Gulf Coast* Poetry Prize, the 2008 Milton-Kessler Memorial Prize from *Harpur Palate*, the 2008 Yellowwood Poetry Prize from *Yalobusha Review*. He teaches writing at Virginia Commonwealth University.

KAREN RIGBY received a 2007 literature fellowship from the National Endowment for the Arts. *Savage Machinery,* her second chapbook, is available from Finishing Line Press.

ANNE MARIE ROONEY is an M.F.A. candidate at Cornell University. Her poetry has appeared in *Pleiades, Ninth Letter, Octopus, Lit, Subtropics,* and elsewhere.

ZACH SAVICH is a graduate of the University of Washington and the Iowa Writers' Workshop. His poems and essays have appeared in *jubilat, The Kenyon Review, Denver Quarterly,* and other journals. His first book, *Full Catastrophe Living,* won the 2008 Iowa Prize. He is an editor of *Thermos Magazine.*

CHARLOTTE SAVIDGE grew up in the Napa Valley and has lived most of her adult life in Brooklyn, New York, where she currently resides. She is a student at the Writer's Studio, and her poems have appeared in *The New York Quarterly* and on the *Prairie Home Companion* Web site.

WILL SMILEY's poetry has appeared or is forthcoming in *Colorado Review, Fence, The Iowa Review,* and others. He is a graduate of the Iowa Writers' Workshop.

S.E. SMITH is a Michener Fellow at the University of Texas at Austin, where she studies poetry and fiction. Her work has appeared in *Black Warrior Review, the Beloit Poetry Journal, Makeout Creek, Ninth Letter,* and *Swink,* among others. Recently, her collection of short fiction was named a finalist in the Keene Prize for Literature.

ETHAN STEBBINS is building a stone archway in East Baldwin, Maine.

ALEXANDRA TEAGUE is a former Stegner Fellow and holds an M.F.A. from the University of Florida. Her work has recently appeared on *Slate,* in *Poetry Daily Essentials 2007,* and in *Notre Dame Review, Epoch, The New England Review,* and *The Iowa Review.* She teaches English at City College of San Francisco.

RHETT ISEMAN TRULL received her M.F.A. from the University of North Carolina at Greensboro, where she was a Randall Jarrell Fellow. Her poetry has appeared in many journals including *Bat City Review, Iron Horse Literary Review, Prairie Schooner,* and *Zone 3.* She is the editor of *Cave Wall.*

ANGELA VOGEL Angela Vogel received the 2008 Southeast Review Poetry Prize and a Maryland State Individual Artist Grant for poetry. Her poems appear or are forthcoming in *The National Poetry Review, Natural Bridge, The Southeast Review, Barrow Street, POOL, RHINO, Pebble Lake Review,* and *Southern Poetry Review.* Her chapbook, *Social Smile,* was published by Finishing Line Press in 2004. She holds an M.F.A. in creative writing from the University of Maryland and publishes *New Zoo Poetry Review.*

Presently teaching at Virginia Commonwealth University in Qatar, DIANA WOODCOCK worked nearly eight years in Tibet, Macau, and on the Thai-Cambodian border. In 2008 she received two awards from Artists Embassy International and a Summer Literary Seminars/Russia Select Scholarship. She's been awarded residencies at MICA/Rochefort-en-Terre, Vermont Studio Center, Virginia Center for the Creative Arts, and in the Everglades National Park. Her poems have appeared or are forthcoming in *Crab Orchard Review, Nimrod, Atlanta Review, Wisconsin Review, Hawai'i Pacific Review, Litchfield Review,* and other journals, as well as in numerous anthologies.

JOSEPHINE YU is a Ph.D. student at Florida State University. Her poems and interviews with writers have appeared in the *Beloit Poetry Journal, 32 Poems, The Southeast Review, River City, Gettysburg Review, Kalliope,* and *The South Carolina Review.*

Participating Writing Programs

University Creative Writing Program
Arizona State
Creative Writing
Tempe, AZ 85287

Master of Arts in Creative Writing
Boston University
236 Bay State Road
Boston, MA 02215
www.bu.edu/writing

Middlebury College
The Bread Loaf Writers' Conference
Kirk Alumni Center
Middlebury, VT 05753
www.middlebury.edu

M.F.A. Program in Creative Writing
Brooklyn College
Department of English
2900 Bedford Avenue
Brooklyn, NY 11210

Program in Literary Arts
Brown University
Box 1923
Providence, RI 02912
www.brown.edu/Departments/Literary_Arts

Creative Writing Program
Colorado State University
Department of English
359 Eddy Building
Fort Collins, CO 80523-1773

School of the Arts
Columbia University Writing Division
Dodge Hall
2960 Broadway, Room 400
New York, NY 10027-6902

Creative Writing Program
Inland Northwest Center for Writers
501 N Riverpoint Blvd Suite 425
Spokane, WA 99202
ewumfa.com

M.F.A. in Creative Writing
Emerson College
120 Boylston Street
Boston, MA 02116-1596

Writing Fellowship
Fine Arts Work Center in Provincetown
24 Pearl Street
Provincetown, MA 02657
www.fawc.org

M.F.A. Program in Creative Writing
Florida International University
Department of English, Biscayne Bay Camp
3000 N.E. 151st Street
North Miami, FL 33181

Department of English
Florida State University
Williams Building
Tallahassee, FL 32306-1580
english.fsu.edu/crw

Creative Writing Program
George Mason University
4400 University Drive
MS 3E4
Fairfax, VA 22030
creativewriting.gmu.edu

Creative Writing Program
Hollins University
P.O. Box 9677
Roanoke, VA 24020

M.F.A. Program in Creative Writing
Hunter College
English Department
695 Park Avenue
New York, NY 10065
www.hunter.cuny.edu/creativewriting

Writing Program
Kalamazoo College
English Dept.
1200 Academy St.
Kalamazoo, MI 49006
www.kzoo.edu/programs/?id=12

Creative Writing Program
Kansas State University
Department of English
108 ECS Building
Manhattan, KS 66506
www.ksu.edu/english/programs/cw.html

Asian American Poetry Retreat
Kundiman
245 Eight Avenue, #151
New York, NY 10011

English Department
Louisiana State University
260 Allen
Baton Rouge, LA 70803
english.lsu.edu/dept/programs/creative_writing

Program in Creative Writing
McNeese State University
P.O. Box 92655
Lake Charles, LA 70609
www.mfa.mcneese.edu/

Creative Writing Program
Minnesota State University, Mankato
230 Armstrong Hall
Mankato, MN 56001
www.english.mnsu.edu

Graduate M.F.A. in Poetry
New England College
24 Bridge Street
Henniker, NH 03242

Department of English
New Mexico State University
Box 30001
Department 3E
Las Cruces, NM 88003-8001
www.nmsu.edu

Graduate Writing Program
The New School
66 West 12th Street, Room 505
New York, NY 10011

Graduate Program in Creative Writing
New York University
58 W. 10th St
New York, NY 10011

Creative Writing Program
Ohio State University
Department of English, 421 Denney Hall
164 West 17th Avenue
Columbus, OH 43210-1370

M.F.A. Creative Writing Program
Old Dominion University
5th floor, Batten Arts and Letters Building
Hampton Boulevard
Norfolk, VA 23529
www.luisaigloria.com

Master of Fine Arts in Creative Writing
Pacific University
2403 College Way
Forest Grove, OR 97116
www.pacificu.edu/as/mfa

M.F.A. in Creative Writing
Pennsylvania State University
Department of English
S. 144 Burrowes Building
University Park, PA 16802

M.F.A. Program
San Diego State University
Department of English and
    Comparative Literature
5500 Campanile Drive
San Diego, CA 92182-8140

Master of Fine Arts Program
San Diego State University
Department of English and Comparative
Literature
San Diego, CA 92182

Office of Graduate Studies
Sarah Lawrence College
1 Mead Way
Bronxville, NY 10708-5999

Sewanee Writers' Conference
735 University Avenue
Sewanee, TN 37383-1000
www.sewaneewriters.org

Program in Creative Writing
Syracuse University
Department of English
401 Hall of Languages
Syracuse, NY 13244-1170

Creative Writing Program
Texas A&M University
Deptartment of English
Blocker 227
College Station, TX 77843-4227

M.F.A. Program in Creative Writing
Texas State University
Department of English
601 University Drive, Flowers Hall
San Marcos, TX 78666
www.txstate.edu

Creative Writing Program
Texas Tech University
English Department
TTU
Lubbock, TX 79409-3091
www.english.ttu.edu/cw/

Program in Creative Writing
University of Alabama
Department of English
P.O. Box 870244
Tuscaloosa, AL 35487-0244
www.as.ua.edu/english/08_cw/index.html

Fairbanks Program in Creative Writing
University of Alaska
Department of English
P.O. Box 755720
Fairbanks, AK 99775-5720
www.uaf.edu/english

Creative Writing Program
University of Arizona
Department of English
Modern Languages Bldg. #67
Tucson, AZ 85721-0067
cwp.web.arizona.edu

Program in Creative Writing
University of Arkansas
Department of English
333 Kimpel Hall
Fayetteville, AR 72701
www.uark.edu/depts/english/PCWT.html

Graduate Creative Writing Program
University of California, Davis
Department of English
Davis, CA 95616

Creative Writing Program
University of Denver
Department of English
2140 South Race Street
Denver, CO 80208
www.du.edu/english/gradcwr.html

Creative Writing Program
University of Florida
Department of English
P.O. Box 11730
Gainesville, FL 32611-7310
www.english.ufl.edu/crw/

Creative Writing Program
University of Hawaii
English Department
1733 Donaghho Road
Honolulu, HI 96822
www.english.hawaii.edu/cw

Creative Writing Program
University of Houston
Department of English
R. Cullen 229
Houston, TX 77204-3015

Creative Writing Program
University of Idaho
Department of English
Moscow, ID 83843-1102
www.class.uidaho.edu/english/
   CW/mfaprogram.html

Creative Writing Program
University of Maryland
Department of English
3119F Susquehanna Hall
College Park, MD 20742
www.english.umd.edu/programs/CreateWriting

M.F.A. Program for Poets and Writers
University of Massachusetts
452 Bartlett Hall
130 Hicks Way
Amherst, MA 01003-9269
www.umass.edu/english/eng/mfa

M.F.A. Program in Creative Writing
University of Michigan
Department of English
3187 Angell Hall
Ann Arbor, MI 48109-1003

Program in Creative Writing
University of Missouri-Columbia
Department of English
107 Tate Hall
Columbia, MO 65211
www.missouri.edu/~cwp

Master of Fine Arts in Creative Writing
Program
University of Missouri-St. Louis
Department of English
8001 Natural Bridge Road
St. Louis, MO 63121
umsl.edu/~mfa

M.F.A. Writing Program
University of North Carolina, Greensboro
3302 HHRA
P.O. Box 26170
Greensboro, NC 27402-6170
www.uncg.edu/eng/mfa

Department of English
University of North Texas
P.O. Box 311307
Denton, TX 76203-1307
www.engl.unt.edu/grad/grad_creative.htm

Creative Writing Program
University of Notre Dame
356 O'Shaughnessy Hall
Notre Dame, IN 46556-0368
www.nd.edu/~alcwp/

M.F.A. Program
University of South Carolina
Department of English
Columbia, SC 29208

Michener Center for Writers
University of Texas
J. Frank Dobie House
702 East Dean Keeton Street
Austin, TX 78705
www.utexas.edu/academic/mcw

Creative Writing Program
University of Texas at Austin
1 University Station B5000
English Department
Austin, TX 78712

Creative Writing Program
University of Utah
255 South Central Campus Drive
Room 3500
Salt Lake City, UT 84112

M.F.A. Program in Creative Writing
University of Virginia
P.O. Box 400121
Chearlottesville, VA 22904-4121
www.engl.virginia.edu/creativewriting

Creative Writing Program
University of Washington
Box 354330
Seattle, WA 98195-4330

Department of English
University of West Florida
11000 University Parkway
Pensacola, FL 32514
www.uwf.edu/panhandler

Creative Writing Program
University of Wisconsin-Milwaukee
Department of English
Box 413
Milwaukee, WI 53201

Creative Writing Program
University of Wyoming
Department of English
P.O. Box 3353
Laramie, WY 82071-2000
www.uwyo.edu/creativewriting

Unterberg Poetry Center/Writing Program
92nd Street Y
1395 Lexington Avenue
New York, NY 10128
www.92Y.org/poetry

Master of Fine Arts in Writing
Vermont College
36 College Street
Montpelier, VT 05602
www.tui.edu

M.F.A. in Creative Writing Program
Virginia Commonwealth University
Department of English
P.O. Box 842005
Richmond, VA 23284-2005

M.F.A. Program
Virginia Tech
English Department
Blacksburg, VA 24061
www.english.vt.edu/graduate/MFA

Weslyan University
Wesleyan Writers Conference
294 High Street, Room 207
Middletown, CT 06459
www.wesleyan.edu/writers

Creative Writing Program
West Virginia University
Department of English
P.O. Box 6296
Morgantown, WV 26506-6269
www.as.wvu.edu/english/

M.F.A. in Professional Writing
Western Connecticut State University
181 White St.
Danbury, CT 06470
www.wcsu.edu/writing/mfa

Graduate Program in Creative Writing
Western Michigan University
Department of English
6th Floor Sprau
Kalamazoo, MI 49008-5092

Canada

Sage Hill Writing Experience
Box 1731
Saskatoon, SK S7K 3S1
www.sagehillwriting.ca

Creative Writing Program
University of British Columbia
Buchanan E462-1866 Main Mall
Vancouver, BC V6T 1Z1
www.creativewriting.ubc.ca

Creative Writing Research Group (CWRG)
University of Calgary
English Department
Creative Writing Program
Calgary, AB T2N 1N4
www.english.ucalgary.ca/creative

Participating Magazines

32 Poems Magazine
P.O. Box 5824
Hyattsville, MD 20782
www.32poems.com

42opus
P.O. Box 311
New York, NY 10276
www.42opus.com

AGNI
Boston University
236 Bay State Road
Boston, MA 02215
www.bu.edu/agni

Alligator Juniper
Prescott College
220 Grove Avenue
Prescott, AZ 86301
www.prescott.edu/highlights/alligator_juniper

The Antioch Review
Antioch University
P.O. Box 148
Yellow Springs, OH 45387
www.review.antioch.edu

Arts & Letters
Georgia College & State University
Campus Box 89
Milledgeville, GA 31061
al.gcsu.edu

Bamboo Ridge:
    Journal of Hawaii Literature and Arts
P.O. Box 61781
Honolulu, HI 96839-1781
www.bambooridge.com

Bat City Review
The University of Texas at Austin
Department of English, The University of
Texas at Austin
1 University Station B5000
Austin, TX 78712

Bellevue Literary Review
NYU School of Medicine
Department of Medicine
550 First Avenue, OBV-A612
New York, NY 10016
www.BLReview.org

Bellingham Review
Western Washington University
MS-9053
Bellingham, WA 98225
www.wwu.edu/~bhreview

Beloit Poetry Journal
The Beloit Poetry Journal Foundation, Inc.
P.O. Box 151
Farmington, ME 04938
www.bpj.org

Black Warrior Review
University of Alabama
Box 862936
Tuscaloosa, AL 35486
www.webdelsol.com/bwr

Blackbird
Virginia Commonwealth University
Department of English
PO Box 843082
Richmond, VA 23284-3082
www.blackbird.vcu.edu

Boston Review
35 Medford Street
Suite 302
Somerville, MA 02143
bostonreview.net

Boxcar Poetry Review
401 S. La Fayette Park Pl. #309
Los Angeles, CA 90057
www.boxcarpoetry.com

Calyx,
  A Journal of Art and Literature by Women
P.O. Box B
Corvallis, OR 97339
www.calyxpress.org

The Carolina Quarterly
University of North Carolina
Greenlaw Hall CB#3520
University of North Carolina
Ghapel Hill, NC 27599-3520

Cave Wall
Cave Wall Press, LLC
P.O. Box 29546
Greensboro, NC 27429-9546
www.cavewallpress.com

Coconut
2331 Eastway Road
Decatur, GA 30033
www.coconutpoetry.org

Colorado Review
Colorado State University
The Center for Literary Publishing
9105 Campus Delivery / Dept. of English
Fort Collins, CO 80523
coloradoreview.colostate.edu

Contrary
3114 S. Wallace Street, Suite 2
Chicago, IL 60616
www.contrarymagazine.com

The Cream City Review
University of Milwaukee-Wisconsin
Department of English
P.O. Box 413
Milwaukee, WI 53201
www.uwm.edu/Dept/English/ccr

Dappled Things
5850 Cameron Run Terrace, # 516
Alexandria, VA 22303
www.dappledthings.org

The Eleventh Muse
Poetry West
P.O. Box 2413
Colorado Springs, CO 80901
www.poetrywest.org/muse.htm

Fence
Science Library 320/University at Albany
1400 Washington Avenue
Albany, NY 12222
www.fenceportal.org

FIELD
Oberlin College Press
50 North Professor Street
Oberlin, OH 44074
www.oberlin.edu/ocpress

Gertrude
Gertrude Press
P.O. Box 83948
Portland, OR 97283
www.gertrudepress.org

The Gettysburg Review
Gettysburg College
300 N. Washington Street
Gettysburg, PA 17325-1491
www.gettysburgreview.com

The Greensboro Review
University of North Carolina, Greensboro
M.F.A. Writing Program
3302 Hall for Humanities and
    Research Administration
Greensboro, NC 27402-6170
www.greensfororeview.org

Guernica: A Magazine of Art & Politics
403 E69th Street #3D
New York NY 10021
www.guernicamag.com

Harvard Review
Harvard University
Lamont Library
Cambridge, MA 02138
hcl.harvard.edu/harvardreview

The Hudson Review
684 Park Avenue
New York, NY 10065
www.hudsonreview.com

I M A G E
3307 Third Avenue West
Seattle, WA 98119
www.imagejournal.org

In Posse Review
4128 Mississippi St # 4
San Diego, CA 92104
webdelsol.com/InPosse

Indiana Review
Indiana University
Ballantine Hall 465
1020 E. Kirkwood Ave.
Bloomington, IN 47405-7103
www.indianareview.org

The Iowa Review
University of Iowa
308 EPB
Iowa City, IA 52242-1408
www.uiowa.edu/~iareview

The Kenyon Review
Kenyon College
Walton House
Gambier, OH 43022-9623
www.kenyonreview.org

Ledge Magazine
Ledge Magazine and Press
40 Maple Avenue
Bellport, NY 11713
www.theledgemagazine.com

The Massachusetts Review
University of Massachusetts
South College
Amherst, MA 01003
www.massreview.org

Memorious:
   A Journal of New Verse and Fiction
12 Laurel St.
Cambridge, MA 02139
www.memorious.org

Michigan Quarterly Review
University of Michigan
3574 Rackham Bldg.
915 East Washington St.
Ann Arbor, MI 48019-1070
www.umich.edu/~mqr

Mid-American Review
Bowling Green State University
Department of English
Box W
Bowling Green, OH 43403
www.bgsu.edu/midamericanreview

The Minnetonka Review
P.O. Box 386
Spring Park, MN 55384

Mississippi Review
The University of Southern Mississippi
Box 5144
Hattiesburg, MS 39406-0001
www.mississippireview.com

Natural Bridge
One University Blvd.
St. Louis, MO 63121

New Letters
University of Missouri-Kansas City
5101 Rockhill Road
Kansas City, MO 64110
www.newletters.org

New Orleans Review
Loyola University
Box 195
New Orleans, LA 70118
www.loyno.edu/~noreview

Nimrod
The University of Tulsa
800 S. Tucker Dr.
Tulsa, OK 74104-3189
www.utulsa.edu/nimrod

Ninth Letter
234 English, University of Illinois
608 S. Wright St.
Urbana, IL 61801
www.ninthletter.com

Northwest Review
University of Oregon
369 PLC
University of Oregon
Eugene, OR 97403
nwr.uoregon.edu

Phoebe
George Mason University
4400 University Drive
MSN 2C5
Fairfax, VA 22030-4444
phoebejournal.com

Ploughshares
Emerson College
120 Boylston St.
Boston, MA 02116
www.pshares.org

Poemeleon: A Journal of Poetry
3509 Bryce Way
Riverside, CA 92506
www.poemeleon.org

Poetry International
San Diego State University
Department of English & Comparative
Literature
5500 Campanile
San Diego, CA 92182-8140

Poetry Northwest
4232 SE Hawthorne Blvd
Portland, OR 97215

Quiddity
1500 North Fifth Street
Springfield, IL 62702
www.sci.edu/quiddity

River Styx
Big River Association
3547 Olive Street Suite 107
Saint Louis, MO 63103
www.riverstyx.org

RUNES, A Review of Poetry
PO Box 401
Sausalito, CA 94966
members.aol.com/runes

Salamander
Suffolk University English Department
41 Temple Street
Boston, MA 02114
www.salamandermag.org

Sentence
Firewheel Editions
Box 7
181 White St.
Danbury, CT 06810
www.firewheel-editions.org

Smartish Pace
P.O. Box 22161
Baltimore, MD 21203
www.smartishpace.com

Sou'wester
Southern Illinois University
Department of English Language
    & Literature
Box 1438
Edwardsville, IL 62026-1438
www.siue.edu/ENGLISH/SW

St. Petersburg Review
Box 2888
Concord, NH 03301
www.stpetersburgreview.com

Stirring : A Literary Collection
Sundress Publications
218 Stevens Dr
Hattiesburg, MS 39401
www.sundress.net/stirring

Subtropics
University of Florida
English Dept. PO Box 112075,
Gainesville, FL 32611
www.english.ufl.edu/subtropics

The Southeast Review
Florida State University
English Department
Tallahassee, FL 32306
www.southeastreview.org

upstreet
Ledgetop Publishing
P.O. Box 105
205 Summit Road
Richmond, MA 01254-0105
www.upstreet-mag.org

The Virginia Quarterly Review
University of Virginia
One West Range
P.O. Box 400223
Charlottesville, VA 22904
www.vqronline.org

The Yale Review
Yale University
PO Box 208243
New Haven, CT 06520-8243

ZYZZYVA
P.O. Box 590069
San Francisco, CA 94159-0069
www.zyzzyva.org

Canada

*Apple Valley Review: A Journal of
    Contemporary Literature*
c/o Queen's Postal Outlet
Box 12
Kingston, ON K7L 3R9
www.applevalleyreview.com

Event
Douglas College
Box 2503
New Wesminster, BC V3L 5B2
event.douglas.bc.ca

Room of One's Own
P.O. Box 46160
Station D
Vancouver, BC V6J5G5
roommagazine.com